Desert Years

UNDREAMING
THE
AMERICAN
DREAM

Cynthia Rich

is also the co-author of

Look Me in the Eye:

Old Women, Aging and Ageism

Cynthia Rich
Desert Years

UNDREAMING
THE
AMERICAN
DREAM

spinsters | *aunt lute*
SAN FRANCISCO

First Edition

10-9-8-7-6-5-4-3-2-1

Spinsters/Aunt Lute Book Company
P.O. Box 410687
San Francisco, CA 94141

The chapter "Roots in the Sand" first appeared in a slightly different fashion in OUT/LOOK, National Lesbian and Gay Quarterly, Issue 6, Fall 1989

Cover and Interior Illustrations: Karen Sjöholm

Cover and Text Design: Pam Wilson Design Studio

Typesetting: Comp-Type, Inc., Fort Bragg, CA

Production: Eileen Anderson   Daniel Bao
                Tita Caldwell   Martha Davis
                Debra DeBondt   Ellen Doudna
                Laura Jiménez   Brenda Kennard
                Deborah Leighton   Madeleine Lim
                Nicole Livingston

Printed in the U.S.A.

Library of Congress Cataloging-in-Publication Data
Rich, Cynthia.
    Desert years: undreaming the American dream/
by Cynthia Rich. — 1st ed.
        p. cm.
    ISBN 0-933216-69-6 (hbk.) : $17.95.
    ISBN:0-933216-67-X (pbk.) : $7.95
    1. Rich, Cynthia. 2. California—Biography. 3. Aged
women—Psychology. 4. Deserts—California. I. Title.
CT275.R534A3 1989
979.4'053'092—dc20   89-35667
                                                 CIP

For Barbara

without whom my life would have been written

very differently

and for all the desert women

Introduction

"But Barbara, this is crazy, we can't live in a trailer. Besides, where would we put our books?"

It is the fall of 1982, and for the past year we have lived in Nashua, New Hampshire. I am working as a software editor for Digital, making more money than I ever made before, learning more than I ever planned to about the World of the Future. But I am not finding much spare life. Even when we moved across the state line because there were no more teaching jobs in Massachusetts, we never meant to stay. We found no pleasure in Nashua's new "prosperity"—those fast-food chains and hastily built condos that were eating up the woods and farmlands. I just wanted training for some skill that wasn't teaching, and a salary to salt

1

away until we could think of what to do next.

Now Barbara has come up with the what next, and I am staring across the dining table into her blue eyes. She has told me a lot about this place in the desert, two and a half hours by car from San Diego, where she and Ethel, a former lover, camped for a few weeks once in the early 1970s. Since Ethel moved to San Diego, Barbara has flown out to visit a few times, and they've spent weekends on the desert in Ethel's trailer.

"The desert" is a county park in the middle of the 260,000-acre Anza-Borrego Desert State Park, and Barbara has let me feel its excitement and peace. I know that the sky every day is bluer than in Cambridge in the fall, that the Vallecito Mountains are grey and purple but turn rosy gold at sunrise and sunset, that the full moon on the sand shines a light you can read by, and that at night the coyotes yap and howl just outside your trailer door.

A few of the 125 campsites are rented year-round by old women and men who have brought a doctor's permit to say that the pure dry air and warm mineral springs will improve their health. Some have stayed for almost twenty years. Most live in trailers, though there are still four small mobile homes from the 1960s when there were forty of these "permittees," almost a tiny town.

Now Barbara is back from another visit. This time she spent a week alone in the camp with pup tent, chair, radio, some firewood and a hamper of food. This time she is suggesting we live there.

2

I've known desert country from New Mexico, so I don't wonder how the idea occurred to her. And certainly we could get a permit, for it's true that the dry air helps the osteoarthritis in her neck.

But the place she describes is very remote and of course hot, and how could we live in a trailer? Even in the city apartments we can feel invaded by the other's presence. Where would we keep our books?

"We could try it for a year, see how little we could live on." Barbara was a social worker before she retired, and once had a job preparing long-time mental patients to leave the institution. She's told me that when the leap into the unknown seemed too terrifying, it could help to partialize it. Maybe it's the same technique, but a year does feel less intimidating. If we could cut expenses, buy a used trailer for $2000, rent a campsite for $150 a month, including utilities— maybe I could free myself, for awhile anyway, from pleasing an employer whose goals have nothing to do with mine.

It would be hard to uproot ourselves from past and present lives. To leave people we love, the excitement of women's political work in New England, feels wrenching. Barbara would lose her writing support group, and I would say goodbye to the first job I ever had that convinced me I could "make it" enough to ensure my survival.

But something deep draws us towards that trailer. We live uneasily in this consumer culture. We don't find many words for the ways it coarsens and cheapens us, though Barbara once said: "I never forget that everything I buy represents time out of the lives of the people who made it." We almost bought a house once, and the night before we were to make our deposit, we sat at another dinner table, surprised by our sudden drawing back. It struck us then that all the messages of society would tell us we were good people for fixing a patch in the ceiling, repairing cellar stairs, painting and pruning. Yet very little outside ourselves rewards us for the time we spend thinking, writing, talking, searching out the truths of our lives. We saw that to buy a house meant to clutter our heads with products. And that to have a head cluttered with products is to be an obedient American citizen.

So the idea now of stripping away more layers of consumerism appeals to us for economy, but not just for economy. Now on the edge of our 50th and 70th years, do we dare to live out a life more in touch with who we think we are?

This is the story from my journal entries during the first three years on the desert. They lay in the trailer cupboard, feeling too personal though I wrote them to share, until the summer of 1988. That was the summer when sun-scorched crops and air thick with pollution forced the media to at last alert people to the greenhouse effect, the same summer when beaches were closed because of dangerous waste tossed up on the shores.

Neither of the empty men who ran for President in this summer of 1988 even touched on how radically we must change our lifestyles, our values, our economic theories if we are to survive at all. And I thought that was not only for the major fear of alienating

4

corporate industry, but also for fear of us, the American public, because corporations have so sold us the magic of progress through technology. To dismember what has been our central myth since the Industrial Revolution, or to give us a firm grasp on how we must now transform our lives, is not to be dreamed of politically. Even in this emergency.

I decided that this record of our experiment might serve not just as one more cry to save the environment, but much more as a small base for hope. We need hope if we are to begin to rename progress. We need to undream the American dream before we can dream it differently.

Finding Our Place

Except for three or four tiny stores, scattered throughout 100 miles of desert, that sell propane, milk and marshmallows, we live a long way from the world of commerce.

Forty miles to the west—4000 feet up the hairpin curves of Banner Grade—is the little mountain town of Julian, its main street three blocks long. The people who live there, or come from San Diego in brief hordes to buy apples from the orchards in autumn or to show the children their first glimpse of snow, all are white. A Black family of freed slaves, the Robinsons, built and operated the Julian Hotel in the late 1800s, but Barbara and I never found their names among the old stones in the Julian graveyard.

Fifty miles to the east is El Centro. Twenty minutes from the border, it's part crumbling frontier town, part McDonald's, Burger King, Thrifty, Sears, Safeway. Spanish floats through the malls, Mexican-American women and their children shop for jicama, Oreo cookies, chilies and soda pop. But the day we ate lunch at the Senior Citizen's Center, almost all the faces were white. We learned that two years ago the Center was moved from the Catholic Church on the Mexican side of town to the new senior housing project on the Anglo side of town.

On the outskirts of our camp, near the mailboxes, John and Vi run one of the tiny desert stores. Like the others, it mainly serves the needs of campers—firewood, beer, popsicles, candy, postcards, ice, a few cans of soup or beans—still, it's oddly reassuring to know it's there. They came a year before we did, to build up social security, when John lost his job at 59. Our first summer here we were business folk, opening the store for a few hours each week while John and Vi were on vacation. But that was just to meet some regulation for their liquor license. We sat in the dark store under the whir of the swamp cooler and nobody came. I had so little practice, I kept forgetting how to use the cash register, and once ran up thousands of dollars for a can of soda pop. But on a spring weekend when the camp is full, Vi and John make $1000, and John stores trailers and tows them in and out of camp for a bit more income.

When Barbara and I drive back from the towns after a meeting or a grocery run, talking politics or prices, we fall into silence. The land opens out around us. Vast stretches of spiny ocotillo, tall barrel cactus, dark creosote bushes shine in the sunshine and clear

8

air, spreading flat on either side of the road for a few miles before beginning a steep climb to form foothills and mountains. On the way from El Centro, we over-look bleached badlands where even the sparse desert rain refuses to fall, then washes flowing with grey-leafed smoke trees and lavender bushes. Coming from Julian, the rounded peaks of the Lagunas shoulder each other, trading shadows back and forth in the shifting light.

Our trailer faces onto such a desert valley, out towards the rosy purple Vallecito Mountains three miles beyond. It sits at the foot of a squat hill on which cluster a dozen trailers and mobile homes of the others who choose this camp for their home. Behind us rise the white, flaky shale folds of the low Tierra Blancas, with their caves and canyons. Looking out our windows in the silence of most days, we can believe we are here alone with the desert. Almost we are.

Twice a day the ranger circles the camp in his truck. Two days each month, at eight o'clock, the little brown and white rural bus passes by to take pas-sengers seventy miles away, past Julian, past Ramona, to the great city malls of El Cajon. And every day at eleven o'clock the roadrunner makes her circuit around our trailer, down the rock wall, across the road to the creosote bushes, back along the campsite and up the rocks again.

Our telephone is a booth in front of the store. At night it's a little oasis of light, glowing against the limitless

9

dark, and sometimes a tarantula will have found its way there first, or one of us will have to beat off the moths or no-see-ems while the other phones. In the daytime the sun presses its heat through the glass. Often it's out of order, and quarters never register properly, so when you use them you have to argue with the operator. But ten years ago there was no telephone for thirty miles, for better or worse.

Barbara and I don't own a TV, which is part of our queerness here; only two stations can cross the mountains anyway. Our radio comes in faintly except for the El Centro station that plays Anglo music all day. Mysteriously, before dawn every day except in midsummer, the *San Diego Union* appears in its blue box at the store, and one or two of them get handed around camp. Our turn comes after Ernie and Eva and before Marie, who does the puzzle. Often we pass it by, because the headlines fill us with disempowering rage, and we learn our news instead from *off our backs, Sojourner, Gay Community News.*

When we first came, I used to carry our wash up the hill to the steel sinks behind the campers' rest rooms. I liked the rhythm of washing and rinsing and using the hand wringer and hanging the clothes on the line, all while I looked out at the drama of Whale Mountain against the brilliant blue sky. I liked that juxtaposition of labor and privilege. I got soft, though, and now we wash socks and underwear by hand in the trailer, sun-drying them on deck chairs, but take our other clothes and the blue double sleeping bag we use instead of bedsheets to a laundromat when we go to town.

We use the trailer's bathtub for storage and walk to the camp showers to bathe. In winter, the spray is cold at first, and you need to wait a few minutes for the warm water to travel from deeper underground. This spring is slightly sulphurous, and when you turn it on the smell is harsh and distinct. But its texture is creamy soft, so a sliver of motel soap lasts a long time. You look up at a strip of sky and mesquite while you lather your body, and the air dries you almost before you need a towel.

The same hot springs feed two large pools, one outdoors with an edge of shade from the desert willows, and an indoor whirlpool spa, not as elegant as the name implies. Up a hill overlooking the camp is a stone pool only a few feet in diameter, of more sulphury waters clear as the desert air, called the "Indian pool," though not so long ago all these springs were part of the territory of the Inyakiipaa Indians. Each of the pools is waist-high, intended not for swimming but for soaking painful limbs in the curative waters.

In the summer, when campers no longer come and even those of us who live here dwindle to five or six, the women meet in the outdoor pool after the sun's slipped behind the mountain. The water holds the heat of the sun, but as we lie talking, our bodies feel cool and quieted. Birds and little brown bats swoop down for a drink.

On the hottest days, when nobody's around, Barbara and I climb the hill alone to the Indian pool and

11

lounge naked in the waters, looking across to the mountain ranges through the burning air.

Sometimes our home is as large as the desert, doors and windows flung wide, expanding us to the top of the Vallecitos, opening up to a puffy white cloud or down the washes where the smoke trees grow. Outside and inside are almost one, and I move my yellow writing pads from the kitchen table to the picnic table under the awning without much sense of transition. Making dinner, I slice off a carrot top at the sink and with one step toss it to a rabbit who is sniffing the sand at the front door. Later at night, I look up from my book to meet the shine of raccoon eyes through the screen, checking me out. When Barbara wakes at 2:00 A.M., she takes the starchart I gave her and sits for an hour finding the constellations that flash silver in the black night sky. Or in the morning I'll see her sipping coffee at the outdoor table, the sunrise glowing across her face.

Sometimes we're trapped inside our eight-by-twenty-four-foot trailer walls. When the summer heat is 120°, or even 110°, we shut our windows and doors, drape them with kitchen foil, and turn on the air conditioner. Even so, every surface is hot to the touch—a glass, a pillow, the formica table top. The water from the faucet scalds our hands. Our bodies and minds slow to a dreamlike pace.

Some nights we make love with the door open to the desert and the moonlight floods our bed and we laugh or cry out with joy as though we were the only

people in the world. Sometimes we go months without
lovemaking. In midsummer there's no wish for breast
on breast. Then we might speak curtly for no better
reason than that the heat lops away at excesses like
courtesy, moving us closer to the core of survival.
When winter locks us in with closed doors and windows, we are too indistinct to rediscover each other at
night.

Sometimes we talk for hours as if we'd just met.
Last night we lay awake not wanting to end the conversation we'd begun on the drive home from a
consciousness-raising group on ageism. The younger
women's terror—it rises like sap at every meeting—
has a fastidiousness to it. They see aging as a disease,
and disease disgusts them. Is it just that they are
molded by a WASP culture that divides women from
our bodies? Barbara wonders. Or is it also that they've
never had children, changed smelly diapers, wiped
runny noses, cleaned up vomit? "They bleed, of
course," says Barbara, "but that's so routinized now—
they don't see it as 'incontinence.'" Aging's an earthy
affair, we agree, which is one of its pleasures too. But
this afternoon, when Kate, in her sixties, remarked, "If
I'm sick, I don't just want a dyke home-visitor, I want
somebody who'll empty my bedpan," only Diana,
Filipina-American, laughed and said, "Kate, I'll empty
your bedpan." Barbara and I thought of that last night.

Sometimes one of us says crossly or wistfully,
"We haven't talked for an age." So we drive fifty miles
to a Mexican restaurant or we wander in a desert
canyon, and try to push through whatever wall crept
up while we weren't noticing. The pain of finding

ourselves again can be like walking on wounds. But afterwards we are giddy with relief, and when we come home we might move towards the bed to celebrate that we've made it through one more time.

After a cold night, we hear a crackling as the metal walls of the trailer expand in the morning sun. Those walls become a kind of skin connecting us to the new rhythms we are learning.

In early spring, gales from the west pound the trailer broadside at fifty miles an hour, sometimes ninety. One moment all's silent, the next moment a thundering slap begins a storm that may last three minutes or three days. The wind roars through the dip in the mountains like a train entering a subway station, and our trailer shudders on its pins. After a few days of it, our nerves jangle and clash.

In July or August—sometimes as late as October —the flash floods come. The sun may be shining, when a small cloud passes over, and abruptly the sky turns to slate. The rain is a banging on the trailer roof, and we have to shout to be heard. But before Barbara and I can begin our debate of "should we go up to higher ground?" it's already too late. The road down from Jake's house is a rushing river. We could never make it through.

The first October we spent here put our trailer to test. It was the worst flash flood in recent memory, picking up picnic tables, huge stones, cement fire rings in its wake, and carrying them a quarter of a mile down the desert slope. When it stopped, darkness had fallen, and we heard, in amazement through the stillness, the eerie roaring of powerful waters. Our trailer stood firm, though a couple down the hill had to stuff towels against their door to keep the water out. Ten miles to the east, the road across Carrizo Wash was flooded for months. Campers came to set up tents and picnic chairs overlooking the desert river.

In winter, the rains are a slow and steady tapping, almost as surprising in the desert silence as the hammering downpour of the floods. We've lain awake listening, first to a gentle beat, and then to the plop of water into saucepans. The next day Barbara climbs the ladder with a pail of roof cement, to search for a crack that may be many feet from the dripping. I hold the ladder and hand her spatulas, trying not to be the incurable femme. By now we both know that those sealed places may open again, when the spring winds rip at the roof.

Sometimes when we have just come back to the desert from a workshop on ageism or from speaking at a conference, have just sent out an article to *New Women's Times* or a mailing for a demo, I can trust that we are doing our work in the world, that I am not betraying myself or other women by this search for a saner life. Other days I pace up and down inside myself to the old refrain, "You are not doing enough. With everything in the world that needs to be done, you are doing nothing." Yet even then, something holds me to this choice.

15

By the end of the first year, our home is here. We do not sit down at a table to discuss, to weigh our decision. If there ever was a trial period, we forgot, and it slipped past without our knowing.

The People
We Found

Late morning brings the residents out of their trailers and mobile homes to wait by the rural mailboxes on the road beyond the store. Mostly it's women I find sitting together on the stone bench in the sun or who wander off a bit to check the progress of an early patch of verbena or the nest of a cactus wren. It's here I begin to sort out the "winter people"—couples who come from November to April each year—from the fifteen of us who have year-round permits. We are: six single women, three single men, three married couples, though here at the mailbox it feels more a women's space than that. At 50, I'm the youngest—mostly we are in our mid-sixties to nineties.

It's the women who explore the desert together every afternoon, and I'm pleased and shy when they ask Barbara and me to join their walks. Barbara snatches the time for aloneness. I say yes.

I don't talk much, new girl on the block, waiting with Eva, Madeline or Dee for the beat-up Chevy to bring our letters from Julian, or wandering down a canyon to find the wild celery with Boots, Eva and Marie, but I feel oddly at ease. Though these are the last people to name it that, this is a dykey sort of world. You never see a skirt, and there's laughter about keeping one just in case of a funeral. Almost always the names that pop up in conversation are women's names: friends who live in Julian or Butterfield or Canebrake; "girlfriends" from high school not seen for years but who send birthday or Valentine cards to keep in touch; sisters and nieces; women who lived here for a while who died or moved away. It's as if, after frantic years of playing by the only rules in town, there's the surprise of letting a self resurface who was submerged so many years before.

For it's the story of our lives. Most women know a time, maybe at ten or twelve, when we begin to feel the force of our love for other women and the growth of our own powers. Then we savor the promise of adulthood: we will be daughters no more but independent doers, makers, thinkers. But by puberty, most white middle-class women in my generation were force-fed a wholly different notion of adulthood: be less than you are, more dependent, let others think for you, leave the love of women friends behind you and practice being dutiful to some man. Divorce, widowhood, as well as our own choices, can offer another chance to create our own adulthood, to be nobody's dutiful daughter.

In puberty they warned us that our early passions for women were just a *phase*. But if we live long enough, the time comes when a woman can look back at those years when she linked her fate with men and see them as just a *phase*. On either side stand years when her primary relationships are with women, with herself.

Eva, Marie, Lucille and the others are living that new chance. The chance to come and go with other women without answering to a man, to make all their own decisions, however limited their tiny budgets. Even the women who still are married have seen some slight shift in the imbalance of power—now they are at least as able physically as their husbands, and he is no longer inflated by that unseen workplace that was supposed to justify his dominance. For perhaps the first time they live beside other women who manage with zest without husbands, and it is clear that they are moving towards that day when they too will cast their lot with themselves and with other women.

Like other things, I notice this on the desert but realize I've seen it before. It helps me to understand why, from the time I was in my twenties, I was drawn to friendships with old women. Not knowing why my only two life choices—marriage and work in a man's world—were hateful to me, I could find no way to be. The old women—widows, divorcées, the never-married—I met for lunch or coffee in my twenties and thirties gave me a sense of another way to be a woman, even though I knew no road to get there. Unlike friends my own age, they talked with me not about boyfriends, husbands, children, bosses, but about their own interests, other women, the larger world. These women weren't mother-substitutes or grandmother-substitutes for me. Curious: they were, though I didn't know it at the time, dyke-substitutes.

The desert women seem to find no special interest or glamour in men. They know that women sustain women.

"Mildred's had to go to Oregon to take care of her mother's things, so Vivian's gone to stay with Vaida" is a typical desert sentence. Vivian's back keeps her in a wheelchair most of the time. But for the next weeks she'll help out Vaida, who lives in a small community twenty minutes away, because Vaida not only needs a wheelchair, but also carries an oxygen tank for her emphysema. Meanwhile, Vaida helps other old women by using her telephone to organize workers to unload trucks of surplus cheese and rice in El Centro.

Almost always, the women look to old women. But Renée, a dark-haired, vivid woman in her thirties, comes in to help Vivian lay her new kitchen tiles and stays for a month. She's the daughter of Vivian's best girlfriend, and I can hear the laughter on Vivian's porch in the evening. When Jake stops at the stairs to tease Renée, "Still not married? A pretty girl like you?" she laughs and says, "Never!" but Vivian booms out, "What do you think she is, crazy?"

When Virgie gives a surprise birthday party for Eva in the recreation hall and invites all the women for a pretty luncheon buffet she's labored to create, it seems never to occur to her to invite any of the husbands or bachelors. In the old days, of course, there'd be the excuse that the men were working or tired from working or they wouldn't enjoy bridge or a baby shower. Now it's just accepted that we belong in different worlds.

The rangers, mostly male, stay for a few years and then move on. They don't have much to do with us while they're here, and barely know our names. Eva's friend Carolyn came to see her in midsummer and told Paul at the gate that she was here to visit somebody. "He told her there wasn't nobody here. I guess he figured we was nobody. I don't think those rangers had it in their heads that we was here."

Sons worry at a distance, tiresomely, ineffectually. Their worrying is an insult to the desert women and sometimes can be dangerous. Pearl at 93 used to roam through the washes and take strangers out to show them the huge barrel cactus sprouting fourteen smaller cacti at its base. She tied little strips of white cloth from her quilting to ocotillos and creosote bushes to help her find the way. Sometimes she'd play the guitar and sing to people on her front porch and almost everybody who regularly visited the desert knew Pearl. When we arrived, Pearl's house was empty. She'd fractured her hip while she was visiting her son Joe. "She wanted to come back here, but Joe said no. He didn't seem to know there are people here who could have took care of her. She could have managed." Last year she died in Missouri in a nursing home.

21

The old single men on the desert live lives quite separate from the women or from each other. They "keep busy," repairing the roof, working on their cars, sawing wood for some mysterious improvement to a tiny old trailer, collecting aluminum cans from dumpsters to exchange for money in the city. They don't come to the Spanish and art classes that Mildred holds in the winter at the rec hall, and they don't go walking together in the evening.

The old men, single or married, are background to the women's world. They're less abrasive than the men I've met in cities, less bent on proving who's boss. Changes in the testosterone level? Matt, who at 90 collects tin cans in an old terry bathrobe and hat, with a towel around his neck against the sun, is raising money for Girl Scouts. Though I can't be sure, I suspect at 50 he would have picked the Elks or Little League. Boots' husband, Ray, gallantly packs his arthritic limbs into their four-wheel drive to take several women to a remote foothill we want to explore, then drives to the other side and waits with sweet patience until we have finished our climb. Are they gentled by being a minority in a women's world? Being outsiders to a larger world, as we all are here? Sometimes I think it's because power doesn't mean much here. The one who has power is nature. She gives each of us a value we didn't have in the city, and it has little to do with city values.

It's the campers, not the permittees, who remind us of the terms of heterosexual life. They stream in on weekends and holidays, even Christmas or New Year's. Partly they are endearing as campers are everywhere, driving for hours to arrive on Friday night, setting up their gear on a dark campsite by flashlight. Especially here, where often the winds beat against their tents at night or blow sand into the hot dog rolls at lunchtime, where there's nothing to "do"—no boating, fishing, swimming—only three pools to sit in and a desert to walk in. Some, of course, come in motor homes called "Pinnacle" or "Pace Arrow" or "Ambassador" or "Commander," with double air conditioners and microwaves and TV—Eva, who's lived here for eighteen years, looks, nods, and says, "Well, they sure are roughing it." But more come in tiny trailers, a borrowed U-Haul truck, or most likely in just their old car with a pup tent. There's grit in their choice, and we feel a connection with them, through these proofs that they value the desert as we do.

But the families! Strolling past the campsites is like opening a door to another culture. I hear the male voices booming out from the mixed groups around the bonfires ("And then I told him . . . and so I said . . . "); I watch the women juggle meals and children in their usual dance, while the men sit with their beers as reward for sinking six stakes in the sand the night before.

The children take over the outdoor pool, driving out the old women, screaming their game of "Marco Polo!" over and over again, and splashing mainly for the attention of mothers who stand on the sidelines with pasted-on smiles. Since Barbara pointed it out to me I see it everywhere: how white middle-class moth-

23

ers talk to their children a lot in public, and smile at them a lot, but immediately they will look out to find the eye of some bystander, as if to ask, "I *am* doing it right, am I not?"

As I go past them into the showers, I think how children used to play with each other oblivious of adults, and when they were in the company of adults, they were absorbed spectators. When was this reversed, so that now adult women are the spectators for children, the audience for their play? Probably this turn-around is what old people have meant when they said, "In my day, children were seen and not heard."

On a crowded weekend we'll hear echoes of the violence of the city. Motorcycles roar past with young men in army fatigues. Twenty-year-old male voices chant through the dusk: "Hey Nicky, you're so fine/ Hey Nicky, you're so fine/ Hey, Nicky, wanna fuck your behind." Or we wander up a canyon and find the shells from illegal target practice and tin cans riddled with rat-a-tat.

One evening we come back from shopping and see a long motor home settled in the usually empty campsite next to us. As we pull our grocery bags from the car a voice booms towards us.

"You ladies need help?"

A large balding man in white shorts, with a great beer belly, comes over in bare feet. We say thank you, we're fine, in a tone that says: we mean it.

Throughout the next week, we come to know him and his wife through the open windows. She's small

24

and dark-haired and wornout-looking. We never hear her speak, and she spends most of her time inside. He sits at the picnic table listening to his new cassettes on a stereo player and arranging them endlessly in their case. They're the kind you order from a TV ad— Moussorgsky, Tchaikovsky, Great Musical Moments.

From time to time we hear him:

I tell you things dozens of times but you don't listen to me. How stupid can you be?

Tunafish! But not like you made it last time. I want a real sandwich.

You and your bonehead ideas.

You sit on your ass. You don't do anything anymore.

You're dumb. You're just plain dumb.

We never hear a word from her. All we know of her is what he tells us, all week, several times a day.

But once, he goes to the pool alone. He's no sooner disappeared around the creosote bushes than she comes outside and sits in his place at the picnic table. She pulls Moussorgsky out of the player and sticks in another cassette and starts to paint her nails. It's Loretta Lynn, and she's singing, "Why don't we say Goodbye the way we said Hello?"

When he returns, Moussorgsky is back in the machine.

A year later, we're teaching ourselves how to raise and lower the awning on our new trailer. A voice calls down from the campsite just above us.

"You ladies need help?"

25

Roots in the Sand

      The sand of the Anza-Borrego is good soil for two dykes who are growing old. Here the act of surviving is a celebration, a kind of joyful defiance. Like our aging, like our lesbianism, the desert doesn't cater to men's desires, and so is defined as lacking, as barren and even unnatural. The word "desert" itself is a stigma, like "old bag" or "dried-up lezzie." Men don't see our abundance, our passion, our beauty, our ingenuity.

      Like an aging dyke, the desert thrives by stripping off what's unessential, merely display for others. Maybe we feel shame when we first turn away from the hetero voices that say, "You're too pale without your makeup," or the youth-worship that insists, "You look ghastly with your scalp showing through your hair." But those seeming losses gather excitement and erotic power from their insistence on truth, from inventing new definitions.

Away from the plastic, glass and asphalt world of San Diego, the process of aging shows more clearly as an affirmation of life rather than as a "failing." The creosote bushes that cover the desert have a history far older than the giant redwoods. I can't read the lines on the face of Whale Mountain or the swirls of rose, grey, orange, green on the boulders of the canyons, but they too talk of geological time.

More: this is a country where, to our eye at least, differences of age or even between the living and the dead are muted. Young or old, the quail, rabbit, road-runner, coyote, kitfox, beetle, mourning dove, ante-lope squirrel, bobcat, raven, cricket, lizard choose grey or greyish brown or black to please themselves and others. Their earthy colors are signals of survival, endurance. A bush next to our trailer looks like a mass of dead twigs, but close up we can see dozens of mauve flowers. You have to have lived the seasons through to know which smoke tree or hedgehog cactus is old or dead and which is just resting between the rains.

And then—as if out of that tenacity, just as the new barrel cactus pushes forth from the body of the old or dying one—come the remarkable bloomings.

I'm much more tuned in here than I used to be back east to the fact that spring isn't a date, it's a mix of conditions. After a rain at any time of year, the oco-tillo sprouts green leaves along its grey stalks and even sends out its huge Chinese-red blossoms to the end of its branches, so that when you look across the desert you see red fingers waving at you. And while it's true that back east some springs are more heady than others, this is the first place I've lived where, if things aren't right, spring decides flat out not to come.

But when winter rains have been heavy enough, spring on the desert is a wonder. You can't see most of it from the window of a car; you can't begin to take the measure of it in a day snatched from city life. Every half-acre has its own blossoming shrubs and flowers unfolding at different times, mixing in ways different from those of its neighbors. It goes on for three or four months and you can walk every day and still see flowers you never saw before.

It is flashy and bold—the golden brittle bush covering the mountains, the purple verbena mixed with dandelions spreading out across the desert floor, the brilliant reds and pinks of beaver tail and hedge-hog cactus, the intense purple blues of smoke trees and indigo bushes aswarm with bees, the great gold tassels of the fifteen-foot-tall agave that look like asparagus growing almost as fast as you can watch, the scarlet chuparosa bushes named for the humming-birds that are drawn by the color and stay for the sweetness. There are hillsides of blue and purple lupine and desert poppies and bright rosy purple monkey flowers. But that's just the beginning, for there's more to discover more slowly: the white desert-lily which may have five crystalline blossoms open on one stalk; the pale pink and lavender primroses and bottle brushes; the rarer purple fivespot with five scarlet dots in its cup; the tiny white tidy-tips that mass themselves between the rocks; the tall pale bushes of the desert lavender where birds love to build their nests; and the creamy ghost flowers with their purple dotted throats, which are so hard to find until you see one and realize they are everywhere.

Baba Copper came to visit in springtime and later sent us a jeweler's glass that used to be one of the sacred objects she kept for her meditations. It brings me another world of amazement, as if I could dive down like a fish to explore coral reefs. Instead, I re-enter the desert through the eyes of a bee or butterfly. The least showy flowers, or ones no larger than a pinhead, undergo the most powerful change. Spanish needles, whose tiny flowers look like pale dry clumps of grass, inflate into huge lavender starflowers with great deep purple stamens.

In spring, of course, the migrating birds spend weeks with us, joining our quail and mourning doves and our pair of ravens. Rosy-breasted finches and yellow tanagers and orioles perch between the thorns of the ocotillo, and sometimes we are startled to see a pair of stark white egrets standing in the roadway or hear the cry of a night heron.

The flowering of the desert in spring unfolds with that mix of the inevitable and unexpected, promise and surprise, that marks all creativity. It is wildly beautiful, but short-lived. It is not the desert's message.

We watch the petals, purple and red and gold, dry in the washes and the ants collect them into downy soft mounds at the entrance of their homes. The winds drive the seeds into the sand. Thousands of bees siphon up the nectar and hoard it in caves at the entrance to Moonlight Canyon, where it hangs like heavy bags through the winter. Without that economy, those connections, the spring would be one more gaudy show. After all, in cities, each mall is springtime, abloom yearlong with the throbbing of colors, surprising us with patterns that change almost daily, promising endlessly renewed life. And still it disappoints, consuming our lives instead of offering us provision.

We learn the desert message with relief and wonder. We know it from our aging, too, from watching seasons of change in our bodies, in our lives, but it's a lesson not of age but of life.

The animals know it. When we lived through our first season of rains, we were surprised to see that even in mid-August they don't rush to the new pools to grab abundance while it is there. They know that, in desert time, those pools last only a moment and that life is about the dailiness of survival, not the sudden excess. So deeply do they know this that the roadrunner turns the rock for the bugs beneath, but does not satiate herself with all she finds there; the rabbit nibbles on the saltbush and loves its tender new sprigs, but leaves enough behind; the coyote lives off the rabbit population but eats mesquite pods rather than pursue the last rabbit.

In the same way, we take in the abundant beauty that comes with spring, but learn to space ourselves with the deep, daily joys of the dry seasons.

In the summer the light and the heat are one, and become almost a noise as they gather intensity. Even the shade of a dry bush matters.

I am surprised that everything on the desert makes a difference. A few drops of winter rain, barely heard on our roof, turn the air sharp with the resinous smell of the creosote. A single cloud spreads a tremendous moving shadow across the mountain and the desert floor.

After all the ways I have been discounted or discounted myself—as a child, as a woman, as a lesbian, as a Jew, and now moving towards old—I find myself healing from the desert's measure of life.

Eva, in her red sweater, as she walks along the path to the mailboxes, and the raven calling from a utility pole against the sky stand out on this uncluttered scene with an odd equality. A family of quail marches, not through a field of grass, but across white sand, and the legs of the tiniest fledgling are distinct in their frail strength.

None of us here need signs like: "I may be a welfare mother, but I am somebody." "I may be old, but I am somebody." "I may be disabled, but I am somebody." Here everything is something, and every one of us is somebody.

I see an ad in a magazine for cassette tapes to relax by. A spring meadow, the ocean—so that's where technology has brought us. I laugh and say I'm going to market a tape called Desert Morning, and it will be absolutely silent.

I thought I'd been to silent places before, and I guess I have if it comes to that—but usually some brushing of trees or lakewater blurs the edge. The morning after a blizzard in the country perhaps—but that silence is more an absence, a suppression of energies. Desert silence is a presence, with a throbbing energy, a sweet passion of its own. It excites the same spot in the cortex as music, and it changes your body in the same way. I spend time listening to it as I would music, coming from a world where it is rarer than music.

Once music was in response to silence, complementing it, a counterpoint to it. Now it is in response to noise, growing louder as every year that noise is harder to drown.

Here we are hundreds of miles from a commercial airport, and except for a navy plane every couple of days, there's no sound of airplanes. I realize for the first time how that faraway hum is now a part of what we call silence in our suburbs and countrysides. Sometimes, sitting in our deck chairs on the sand, Barbara and I look up to see a tiny plane headed for the San Diego airport, but it's so distant we wouldn't have known it was there without tilting our heads.

On many days, when I wash my hair, it dries before I can pass a comb through it. After a walk, we drink three glasses of water, barely stopping to breathe. In such a world, the tasteless water from our faucet surprises us with its sweetness. The sulphurous springs of the Indian pool are more an acquired taste, though people say they're more curative. Sometimes in the evenings the desert women will climb the hill to fill our bottles with the clear, sharp-smelling water, as women have all over the world for thousands of years.

Our water is plentiful, at least in balance with those of us who use it. Odd to think that here, in the midst of more than a million acres of desert, these springs flow lavishly, even in summer, while in Boston and San Francisco they argue about how to keep the water trickling through their taps.

During lovemaking, I'm a laugher. The pleasure washes through me and its excess spills out—luckily, so I don't come too soon. I laugh too when Barbara looks at me squarely across our dinette table and says that she loves me. These are not the same laughs as when friends visit and we laugh together about Ronald Reagan or the contradictions in the lesbian community.

Until I put down roots here, I never felt the laughter bubble from my diaphragm just looking out the window at a mountain golden in the morning light, just knowing myself alive and connected to a world that generously includes me.

Laughing, I feel purged of the desolation of my childhood in family, of the loneliness I pursued into my marriage because it was famil-iar.

Joy, not simple contentment, is a revolutionary act. It tells us what power, what rights live in our cells, and it insists that we not settle for less.

The Conversion of the Jews

      No mistaking it, this is a Christian world. Bernie, a retired undertaker, holds services every Sunday in the recreation hall. About seven or eight permittees come and whatever campers Bernie can pull in. A few, like Marie, have always gone to church and enjoy the little ritual of community. Bernie, his wife Marge and several others are Born Again.

      Boots is born again the most. Eva buys a lot of it, the parts that seem to promise the decency and compassion and fairness of Jesus. The others lend her religious tapes and magazines and I sense how she sifts out what's usable.

      One morning soon after our arrival, I find myself in the indoor pool with Bernie and Marge and Eva. Bernie and Marge are at one end and I'm at the other.

Eva is swimming around the center, and I watch the bounce of her shining white hair and the grace of her slim body in her old yellow bathing suit.

"Jerry Falwell's starting up a school up near Alpine." Bernie's voice, directed towards Eva, booms and echoes against the high ceiling.

So there I am.

"Good," says Eva mildly. "We need that."

"Have you heard about the new translation of the Bible? There's an article about it in that magazine I gave you. They want to call God 'Father-Mother' and call Jesus 'The Child' of God."

"The National Council of Churches is behind that," Marge notes, with a hint of the ominous.

"Seems like the ladies are pushing for it," says Bernie.

"Oh, I don't care for that," says Eva, and then she glances at me.

Is Bernie really talking to Eva or to me—does he know I'm a Jew and a 'women's libber'? Does that possibility dawn on Eva too, and is that why she wades over to me and says, "It's fun doing that—swimming with the current. Try it."? She means the current from the jets, but I know there are currents here I can never swim with.

One morning I accept a ride with Boots back from the mailbox. We stop at the ranger station to deliver their mail and Randy, the young ranger with clipped moustache and goatee, comes to my window. Boots talks to him across my lap.

"I wanted to ask—would your wife like some books about the Holy Spirit?"

Randy beams. "Well, she already has a lot of them, but we can always use more. Wanted to invite you for her baptism, but you were away. It was a wonderful day."

"Praise the Lord."

You would think the Holy Spirit had wafted me away, but I'm still sitting there between them, large and unsaved as ever.

"You know," Boots confides as she drives off, "Randy is so happy, his wife has finally accepted the Lord. She resisted for the longest time, but now she's teaching Sunday School."

I'm longing to hear about her resistance, but I know I won't get the real story. Besides, I'm feeling chilled in the noonday sun, and can't wait to climb out of the cage of Boots' van and into the open space of the trailer.

Jake and I are the Jews. In September, Jake will celebrate his nineteenth year in this camp, but there's another camp that after forty years often haunts his nights. He lives, not in a trailer, but in one of the few mobile homes in the park on the little hill in back of us. Sometimes at four in the morning when I straggle to the bathroom, I see the lights from his windows streaming into ours. He's told me that night is when he struggles with the sights and sounds of Buchenwald. He'd been in the Polish army and then in a German prison camp where his fellow soldiers gave him away—for what? Cigarettes? A better week's ration? Onward Christian soldiers.

After the war, he came to Pasadena and set up a furniture-making business. But years later he couldn't breathe and was told the chemicals that he'd been using weren't properly labelled and had eaten his lungs. He wasn't expected to live more than a year, but he came out here and has lived eighteen.

In his short, stocky body his lungs are stronger now but are still the canaries in the industrial mines of progress. Sometimes he drives to San Diego—a city rated "good" on the newspaper's daily arc of air quality. Jake's lungs tell a different story, of rasps and wheezes until he's headed home, well past Ramona. Last month for the first time I saw a muddy strip all along the ocean's horizon at Pacific Beach. I doubt the *San Diego Union* will confirm it, but it's Jake's delicate, tough body that can't be argued with.

Most Holy Days he can't go to services, but he celebrates in his home, wearing what Eva calls with affectionate admiration "his little cap." Eva's been here for eighteen years too, and they've spent many summers as the only ones on the desert except the ranger, living out the blazing heat and sudden flash floods.

People in camp forget that I'm Jewish, as if it will go away if they forget, and I am always reminding them. At the mailbox, Bernie asks, "Are you ready for Christmas?"

"Well, I'm Jewish, you know." I should have added: "So I'm ready for anything."

"I know, I know," Bernie says, meaning he's embarrassed for both of us to have forgotten that unpleasant detail. "But are you ready for Passover?"

"Passover's in the spring, but Chanukah's here already."

Nobody forgets that Jake is a Jew. Maybe it's his "little cap" on Holy Days or his heavy accent, but it's Jake, not I, who stands between the born-again Christians and the promise of their Second Coming. If Jake, and a few million other Jakes, can accept the New Testament, Jesus will descend and fulfill the prophecies. Here on the Anza-Borrego desert, the timeless struggle goes on for the Conversion of the Jews.

Jake shows me the cupboard full of brightly colored Christian magazines that people have given him. Zealous campers, when they hear of the Jew who's lived here eighteen years, feel free to knock on his door to bring him the newer Word of God.

"These religious Christians, I don't trust them," he tells me. "They won't let you alone, they're trying to convert you. When I see the religious medals, I steer clear."

We snort at the "Jews for Jesus" trotted out on evangelical television.

"I met a young woman down at the store, she tells me she's converted. I say to her, 'It won't do any good, because you were born a Jew and when you die, you will die a Jew.'" Jake's denied his Jewishness only once, in prison camp, and it didn't do any good.

"You wouldn't believe the people who come here and pretend they're not Jewish. They don't fool me, of course, and they know I know. I've seen them keep it up for years."

I believe it. I've been there. Or at least I have if there's no difference between pretending and ignoring. I ignored my Jewishness for years, having had no taste of Yiddish or laughter or knishes to ground me, my father crossing his leg over his hand so he wouldn't give himself away with a gesture. I was rootless anyway, odd child out of the family circle. Then repeated, as women often repeat, marrying a man who wanted to ignore his Jewishness and ignore me.

One day as I walk towards the mailbox where Eva, Boots and Jake are standing, I hear Boots asking Jake: "How old a man is he?" and Jake answering: "About 38. He used to be a ranger here."

Boots nods in delight. "Oh—I met him the other day up at Butterfield Ranch. He is a lovely Christian man. His daughter had made pictures of God and Jesus."

Jake doesn't bat an eye. "He wasn't liked much here. He used to go into people's trailers and watch their TVs when they weren't home."

Eva nods. "We used to call him the Boss. Lots of people left because they couldn't take him. We lost a lot of people that way."

Jake doesn't let up. "People said he was recalled. Then he tried to go into business with his brother, but his brother couldn't stand him. And they say he wouldn't help his own mother."

Boots takes a deep breath. "He must be a miserable man. I think I'll put him on our prayer list."

Barbara and I are down at the store, sitting on the wooden picnic table and eating ice cream bars, when a green panelled van pulls up. A stubbly faced, middle-aged man gets out followed by his sons, maybe twelve and fourteen. We don't notice them much but when they come out of the store with their beer and pop, we hear the tight note in Daddy's low voice. He's saying, "We'll hide the can and you won't tell nobody." They take their drinks to the tables in the shade of the tamarisks. But it's not long before a car drives in and pulls up sharp. A man jumps out and starts to chase the father and the kids, shouting, "You know what you did!" to their "We ain't done nothing."

"You stay here till the sheriff comes!" And they do, and so do we, learning from a couple who drive up moments later that huge swastikas have appeared high on the rocks at Indian Gorge, so high you can see them from the main road. I think of Jake, I think of the Indians for whom the mark of the swastika meant the gods of the rains, the mountains, the rivers, and how can the swastika ever mean that again? When the sheriff appears, we tell him what we heard before he goes over to Daddy, who's saying, "We ain't done nothing." Later, when the can of red paint is pulled from the trunk, Daddy says, "Musta been the kids, I know I didn't know nothing about it." And the kids, pale and skinny and sullen, stand there silently, trapped in the space between Daddy and the sheriff.

Once a week between November and April, Barbara and I go to Spanish classes in the recreation hall, taught by Mildred, a woman in her early seventies who lives in a little trailer twenty minutes from here. Our first December, she read stories of the baby Jesus and asked us all to read aloud essays on how we'd be spending Christmas.

Barbara and I each wrote that we never celebrate Christmas, and I added that I am Jewish. In the four years she had taught the class, this was obviously the first time the Christmas assumption was questioned. Predictably, this December Mildred stops by our trailer to ask if I'll write a little essay on Chanukah to read to the class.

Well, of course what I'd hoped was that she'd drop Christmas rather than pick up Chanukah. Ever since Chanukah became the "Jewish Christmas," little kids have been matching their tiny dreidels and chocolates and nine candles to the creche, the carols, Saint Nick, stockings and glittering trees. Or else have been swept into the Madison Avenue dreamworld of endless shoddy gifts. I want no part of this exercise. But what to do?

I only have a day to channel my anger to some useful purpose. In Spanish, too. Finally, I decide that I will take the fact that I am what our friend Ethel calls "a sorry Jew"—with no training in my heritage—and make that for once a bridge instead of a gaping hole.

In the end, in struggling Spanish, this is how it goes:

Porque soy medio judía y medio cristiana (Because I am half Jewish and half Christian), *mi relación a la Navidad es interesante* (my relationship to Christmas is interesting). *Cuando estaba una niña en Baltimore* (When I was a little girl in Baltimore), *mis padres celebraban la Navidad, no Chanukah* (my parents celebrated Christmas, not Chanukah). *Hacían eso porque anti-semitismo, como racismo* (They did this because anti-semitism, like racism), *era muy fuerte en Baltimore* (was very strong in Baltimore). *Por ejemplo, recuerdo ver un letrero sobre una piscina* (For example, I remember seeing a sign above a swimming pool) *Solamente Los Gentiles* (Gentiles Only). *Johns Hopkins Escuela de Médico en donde mi padre era patólogo* (Johns Hopkins School of Medicine where my father was a pathologist) *cuidadosamente acceptó cado año solamente uno o dos estudiantes* (carefully accepted each year only one or two students) *de los muchos judíos muy capacitados que aplicaron* (of the many very capable Jews who applied). *Y mi padre era uno de solamente dos profesores judíos* (And my father was one of only two Jewish professors) *en el hospital grande* (in the large hospital).

Por eso (For this reason), *las presiones de conformarse eran muy fuerte* (the pressures to conform were very strong), *y como las familias cristianas en nuestra vecinidad* (and like the Christian families in our neighborhood), *teníamos un arbol de Navidad grande* (we had a big Christmas tree), *cantábamos los villancios de Navidad* (sang Christmas carols), *enviábamos las tarjetas de Navidad* (sent Christmas cards), *y saludábamos todo el mundo y noso-tros mismos, Felices Navidades* (and wished every-body and ourselves, Merry Christmas).

En casa (At home), *no hablábamos casí nunca tocante del significado de ser judío* (we almost never spoke about the meaning of being Jewish), *porque ambos de mis padres deseaban proteger sus niñas de ser "diferentes"* (because both of my parents wanted to protect their children from being "differ-ent"). *Y nunca hablábamos* (And we never talked) *de porqué celebrábamos las fiestas cristianas y no las fiestas judías* (about why we celebrated the Chris-tian holidays and not the Jewish holidays).

Después de mil novecientos quarenta y cinco (After 1945), *entendí un poco más acerca de porqué* (I understood a little more about why) *mis padres pensaban que necessitaban protegerme* (my par-ents thought it necessary to protect me). *Pero aun después de que me puse adulta* (But even after I became an adult), *yo—como muchos cristianos* (I—like many Christians) *—no entendí porqué los judíos* (—didn't understand why Jews) *muchas veces ten-ían los problemas con las Navidades* (often had problems with Christmastime). *No era así para mi* (It wasn't so for me). *¿Porqué tuvo alguna impor-tancia* (Why was it of the slightest importance) *si hay un nacimiento delante de un edificio cívico* (if there was a creche in front of a public building), *o los villancicos en todas las tiendas* (or Christmas carols in all the stores), *o si la gente decían Felices Navi-dades a todos* (or if people said Merry Christmas to everybody) *sin molestarse por saber si fueron cris-*

tianos (without bothering to know if they were Christian)?

Fué solamente a medida que me puse más vieja (It was only when I was older), *hablé con más amigos judíos* (spoke with more Jewish friends) *y aprendí más de mi historia judía* (and learned more of my history as a Jew), *que yo entendí verdaderamente* (that I really understood). *Y yo pensé que puede ser útil* (And I thought it might be useful) *si alguien que celebraba la Navidad* (if someone who used to celebrate Christmas) —*pero quien también identifica con su historia judía* (—but who also identifies with her Jewish history) —*explique lo que muchas veces embrolla los cristianos durante las Navidades* (—explained something that is often confusing to Christians during the Christmas season).

Aprendí que el problema por los judíos durante las Navidades (I learned that the problem for Jews at Christmastime) *no es la felicidad de que gozan los cristianos durante su fiesta* (isn't the happiness that Christians enjoy during their holiday). *El problema es la suposición* (The problem is the assumption) —*mucho más marcada en las Navidades* (—much more marked at Christmastime) —*que todo el mundo en la sociedad es cristiano* (—that everybody in society is Christian). *Por los judíos* (For Jews) *no es simplemente una cuestión de una negligencia innocua* (it is not just a question of a harmless oversight). *Es una suposición muy peligrosa para ellos* (It is an assumption very dangerous for them). *¿Por qué? Porque repetidas veces* (Why? Because many times) *esa se mezcla con una otro suposición* (this

45

gets mixed with another assumption) —*que todo el mundo* debe *ser cristiano* (—that everybody *should* be Christian).

Siglo tras siglo (Century after century), *en país tras país* (in country after country), *los judíos en primer lugar han sido exhortados a convertirse* (Jews have first been encouraged to convert), *y después* forzados *a convertirse* (and then *forced* to convert). *Y siglo tras siglo* (And century after century) *esa fuerza implicaba brutalidad atroz* (this force involved atrocious brutality), *las matanzas y el homicidio* (massacres and murder).

Puede parecer demasiado tosco (It may seem too harsh) *hablar de las matanzas* (to speak of massacres) *durante las fiestas* (during the holidays). *Pero créo que esos de nosotros que somos cristianos* (But I believe that those of us who are Christian) *desean que la Navidad* (want Christmas) *sea una temporada de paz en verdad* (to be a season of true peace). *La paz verdadera quiere decir el entendimiento* (True peace means understanding) *de los quienes son diferentes de nosotros* (those who are different from ourselves), *y entendemos solamente si tenemos el saber* (and we understand only if we have knowledge).

Los judíos desean que los cristianos gozan de sus fiestas (Jews want Christians to enjoy their holidays), *como ellos gozan de Pesach y Chanukah* (as they enjoy Passover and Chanukah). *Pero ninguna persona puede decir* (But nobody can say) *que los judíos no tienen buenes razones* (that Jews haven't good reasons) *por sentirse amenzados* (to feel threatened) *para aún las suposiciones más inocentes* (by even the most innocent assumptions) *que todo el mundo es cristiano* (that everybody is Christian).

Por eso, yo he aprendido decir "Felices Pascuas" (For this reason, I have learned to say "Happy Holidays") *en vez de "Felices Navidades"* (instead of "Merry Christmas") *a menos que soy muy segura* (unless I am very sure) *que la persona a quien hablo* (that the person I am speaking to) *celebra la Navidad* (celebrates Christmas). *Una temporada de amor y de felicidad* (A season of love and happiness) *debe hacernos especialmente generosos* (should make us especially generous) *y cuidadosos del dolor* (and attentive about the pain) *que podamos sin pensar causar a los otros* (that we may without thinking cause others). *Y aunque tengo a veces tristeza* (And although I am sometimes sad) *porque mi padre no estaba más valeroso* (that my father was not more courageous), *creo que ninguna persona* (I believe that nobody) *debe tener tales razones* (should have such reasons) *para estar intimidado para su diferencia* (for being intimidated by his difference) *que tenía mi padre* (as my father had).

Pues, en este día segundo de Chanukah (So, on this second day of Chanukah), *deseo felices Chanukahes* (I wish happy Chanukah) *a todas las personas que celebran Chanukah* (to everybody who celebrates Chanukah), *felices Navidades a todas las personas que celebran la Navidad* (merry Christmas to everybody who celebrates Christmas), *y felices pascues y la paz a todos* (and happy holidays and peace to everyone).

47

While I'm reading and when it's over, I see change in people's eyes. I believe in that change, even next year when Vi sends us a Christmas card. I know for myself that deep changes, especially changes in my relationship to power, can take years. Until there are changes in structures, both Vi and I will learn much much too slowly.

The pain I've caused other women in the women's movement, and they've caused me, the days when it's felt as if we would never breathe a spontaneous breath or speak a word without questioning its meaning, are the bitter fruit of all the givens that have been carefully seeded in our language, in the forms of our thought. Because once oppressive systems are set up, brute force or even conscious prejudice isn't needed to keep them operating daily. Only business—or Merry Christmas—as usual.

A Death
on the Desert

Boots, Eva, Lillian and I are heading home from our afternoon walk. It's Friday of the first big camping weekend of the spring, and Eva tells us she's seen John towing trailers all day from the storage lot up to the campsites. The store can expect good business—campers crowding in for beer or ice, children trying to finish their Fudgesicles before the sun does.

A helicopter is circling the store and we watch it land in the little parking area by the tamarisks. That means nothing good and we hasten our steps. I can just make out a flame and a burst of smoke. I feel myself braced. Our life here is fragile and interwoven, and we can't indulge in the remote horror of cluckers who stand by at city accidents. As I come nearer, I see a county ambulance, the sheriff's car, the green truck of the park rangers. It's not a fire—the flame must have been a flare for the helicopter—and someone is very ill. Roy, the volunteer ranger, tells us it's John, he's had a heart attack. Vi is in the house, where he's been given oxygen. It took two hours for the helicopter to come, since they wouldn't start out until the sheriff had arrived from Julian to declare the emergency real. No matter that Vi is a retired nurse or even that a fireman friend who is a paramedic was at the house. Rules are rules.

Boots grabs the hands of Lilla and Eva, who looks embarrassed (for me? for herself?), and begins to pray. Nobody takes my hand or Roy's, I'm Jewish and Roy never attends church. I'm sure he's as bemused as I am to be so instinctively excluded as not on proper speaking terms with the Lord. "Dear Lord, Maker of all things, if it is thy will that John, thy servant . . . in the name of your son, Jesus Christ."

Vi comes out of the house to say she knows he's gone, his eyes rolled backwards. We hug her and Boots insists that we mustn't lose hope, but I believe Vi and don't need to wait for the guys, who took so long to get here, to pronounce his death. Some teenagers come to the store and Vi waits on them. Of course, it's only a few minutes before Billy the fireman comes in to tell Vi what she knows: "It's over." The little crowd is getting thicker and I leave, knowing that Vi's not one for lamentations and can use practical support later.

In fact, when I go back an hour or so later, Vi's sent the lamenters home and is telephoning relatives from the store. A ranger and Billy are standing about helplessly. I tell the ranger I'll spend the evening with

Vi and tell Billy to go back to his trailer to eat dinner. Both look grateful.

Vi and I sit in the living room of her mobile home and talk. The sheriff called the Neptune Society who will do the cremation and we're waiting for them to arrive. John's in the bedroom, and all Vi wants is not to see him, so she can remember him alive, and to get him out of the house before his son arrives late tonight. She doesn't want dinner. We talk about today, and Vi tells me about her life with John. They've been together twelve years—first an affair that made Vi break with the Church, then marriage. "Oh, we had our ups and downs, but we had a good time. I know it sounds old-fashioned, but he was a real gentleman." It does sound more old-fashioned than I know Vi to be, but I also know about Vi's first husband, who drank and was brutal and squelched her adventurousness. Compared to him, John's self-conscious courtesy gave her life harmony. She knew he wasn't very bright, that she was the one who really ran the store, did the accounts, figured the taxes.

"He had his faults," Vi is saying. "He was a terrible bigot."

I suspect she's saying that to me because John was never entirely comfortable with us, two independent women whom Vi had undoubtedly informed him must be lesbians. And one of us is a Jew, and our Black friend visits often.

"But he was a good man," she continues, and I believe her *buts,* for her, after the suffering of her first marriage. And John meant access—someone to go to shows with, to explore the countryside with, to go to

51

Vegas with—because, although Vi is pluckier than he was, she is a woman who cannot imagine real "larks" without a man. As for many women, the male smell of John beside her in bed must have meant the promise of a wider life than she could ever hope for as an unmarried woman. How to separate out that magnetism from sexual magnetism or from love? She'd never expected him to live long, she says, not even this long—his whole family has a history of early deaths from heart attacks. "Now it's solo for me," she says, but she's thought about it often enough before so the raw edge of fear is off.

It's dark now and Billy returns. He accepts a whiskey and tries to reset the tone from the reflective and honest to the lugubrious and laudatory.

"John was the greatest. Just the greatest," he extols lamely. That's one thing you can say. The other is: "You know, I can't believe it. I just can't believe it."

He is obviously rattled that Vi is not crying, though he would be equally rattled if she were. But then maybe he could leave her tactfully with her female comforter. Now he has to say "Thank you" for refills of whiskey and try to keep the conversation appropriately grief-stricken without much help from the women whose real job it is to carry that one.

The house telephone is in the bedroom, so I go across to the store to phone the Neptune Society. They're on their way, beyond radio contact, should be here any minute if they don't get lost in the desert night. It's moonless, and I get a flashlight from Vi to wave down what I imagine will be a long black limousine. Instead, as the headlights creep closer, I see an old green hatchback. It pulls in to park, a bearded man in his sixties and a severe woman with cropped grey hair get out. She's pale in her black pants suit and reminds me of some sexist and ageist image of death in a Cocteau film. Later she tells me she gets easily carsick, and her stomach turned upside down taking the curves of Banner Grade.

I tell Vi they're here, and she goes into the store to wait till they've gone. Billy and I help them lift the folding gurney cart from the back of the car and guide it into the living room. We lead them into the bedroom, but it's hard to get through the door because John's big body is on the floor and his feet are in the way. There's a sharp odor in the room, despite open windows and a rotating fan—I don't know enough to tell if it's death or some medicine, and my ignorance startles me. While the Neptune Society woman empties his pockets, I take in John. His eyes are closed but his face and his chest under his open shirt are still ruddy with sun. He looks so healthy and, when I search for a word, real. I feel grateful to him as I never did in life, for sharing this time of transition with me. Alive, he had nothing to tell me except how to set the propane tanks, and that with a fussy self-importance. Now, quite simply and directly, he offers me a piece of life-changing knowledge. The difference between life and death isn't between something and nothing. They are both stages of being. John *is,* and will be tomorrow when he's ashes, and it's this fact that connects us to all being, animate and inanimate. The separations aren't vast at all, and the metamorphosis can happen at any time. Everything's always changing, and we are too, death doesn't stop that, says John.

The Neptune woman is unfastening his belt with the silver clasp, and exposes a bit of John's belly, a startle of white flesh. For an instant he feels vulnerable to me, as if we could hurt him, but it's only another shoring up of the false breach between life and death.

"Who is responsible for keeping these?" asks the Neptune woman, and I take the belt, the money clip, the gold Shriners ring that has just come from his finger. I take them out to the living room and put them on the table for Vi. When I come back, the three of them are lifting John's heavy, rigid body awkwardly in the little space. I guide them out to the gurney, like guiding the movers, except there's nothing to chip. I can hear his weight as they drop him on the cart.

When he's in the hatchback, covered with the green drop cloth, the Neptune people go into the store to get John's social security number and birth-date. Behind the cash register, Vi gives them the numbers, another transaction. In a few minutes, John is travelling through the desert darkness, still in the process of becoming.

In the next weeks, the question "Are you going to sell the store?" makes Vi cross. When Dave says, "It's too hard for you, a woman alone," she tells him: "I've been a working woman all my life and, believe me, I've worked hard. Of all the jobs I've had, this is the easiest." Of course she won't sell the store, not soon anyway. Don't they know she's been running it all along?

On the desert, there's no mistaking the precarious-
ness of all life, the fact that death's only a happen-
stance away. Bones we see rarely since they are
quickly chawed and gulped, but in the night we hear
the coyotes on their rabbit chases, we see the roadrunner stalking her lizard, the raven with the boa in
her mouth. The dead cactus or ocotillo stands out
against the white sand and blue sky, for years still a
part of the scene.

I've come to think we sentimentalize death when
we imagine it as not just the end of life but as if it must
somehow be the summing-up of everything that pre-
ceded, like the last scene of a novel or a film. How we
long for life to have a proper shape and it doesn't.
We're tempted to treat "last wishes" as if they must be
revelations of longings closest to a lifetime's core of
being, while in fact they are only this week's, this
month's wish. We want death to turn up some final
secrets of personality and meaning, and that's a
weight too ponderous for it to bear. I used to write
letters to my children for them to read when I died,
but the letters kept getting outdated.

John and the other desert creatures remind me
that, whether we die at 5 or 105, death doesn't arrive
at our doorstep because we have reached some magi-
cal culmination. One day we stumble in the road and
we're stopped. Because we happen to be on this road
when we stumble doesn't mean we wouldn't have
branched off on to another next week if we'd had the
chance, or found ourselves trudging backwards awhile
as I often do. (The French "reculer pour mieux sauter"

puts a good face on that tiresome backward trek—we retreat so we can make a better leap forward.)

As long as we sentimentalize death, those of us who are younger will probably keep distorting the lives of old women and men, whom we see—not always correctly—as nearer death than we are. It's not just that we set up the impossible demand that they ring with the confident tones of the last chords of a symphony. In expecting them to be "finished" or near-finished, we in fact make them less exciting, more closed to discovery than our own searching selves. Who is so little worth investing in as someone we believe to be no longer open to change?

Naming,
Unnaming,
Staking Claim

The week Barbara camped here in her pup tent, before we came here to live, the desert women noticed her. They brought firewood, took her out to see the giant cactus, explained how to go about getting a permit. One day sitting with them on Pearl's porch, she told them a bit about herself, including that she writes for lesbian feminist newspapers and journals.

What they made of that, we don't know. We haven't used the word *lesbian* since we came, but when we traded our twenty-four-foot trailer for a thirty-one-foot one, we invited all the women in to see it, with its grand double bed.

They call us The Girls. After all the times we've insisted "I'm not a girl," we find we're pleased. Proud, even, to wear the same title as the city of Toronto gave to the two lesbian sculptors who lived and worked together in an abandoned church through the first half of this century—Emily Loring and Florence Wyle, whose sculpture is powerful and whose faces were sculpture.

Sometimes we leave the camp and travel through the desert up to Julian, past Ramona and out to the sea. Every few months I see another of the glowing gold and green rounded hills of Southern California lacquered over with huge new apartment complexes. Seems like everybody wants to live on a mountaintop. On the road to Escondido, a sky-blue billboard shows a single white peak with the words: *The Heights. Aspire.* Climbing is the great American metaphor: if my foot isn't over your head then probably yours will be over mine. Then there are the vast tracts of condominiums that snatch their names from what they have just destroyed: Quail Run, Coyote Canyon, Roadrunner Park, Oak Hill. Like all the hiking trails in the desert called Indian Gorge or Indian Canyon, we exploit the memory of what we've wiped out in reality. And of course to call this rock Indian Rock or that hill Indian Hill implies that there is some rock or hill that wasn't, a very short time ago, part of a 3000-mile-wide Indian Country.

Or we can try to wipe out the reality by changing the name. That happened in Earthquake Valley, twenty-five miles from here, as soon as a few people put up mobile homes there and other people bought lots, dreaming of the desert's commercial future. On the new maps it's Shelter Valley, a nice name to remember when your dishes are rattling.

And a few miles west of Shelter Valley curls the mountain pass towards Julian, Banner Grade. It used to be called America Grade, after America Newton, a freed slave and an "independent woman," so a pamphlet in the Julian library tells me. She homesteaded there, and made her living doing laundry, turning out the finest shirts and ruffles with big tubs and a washboard. Nobody knows just when America was erased and replaced by Banner, for the flag two white men raised to stake their claim to gold.

When you're a child or a young person, the river of time stretches from your first memories to the present. Everything that happened earlier is just the glacial source of your own free-running current. The glacier stopped melting at the time of your birth, and when you squint upriver you see HISTORY, that great icy block. Embedded in it are frozen figures: little soldiers, people in funny togas and loin cloths, horses and carriages, masters and slaves.

After about half a century of living, most of us are aware, if we think about it, that HISTORY is melting rapidly, that those funny little people have washed into our current and don't seem nearly as funny. Yet at the same time it's clear that the whole river isn't very big at all. In a short time we've watched clothes we used to wear become campy, our cars become collector's items. We've seen progress rip up wooden towns and replace them with steel and glass high-rises

59

and malls. We know that we—who have lived so briefly—become ancient and less real when we remind a woman of thirty that we grew up without television.

I had a preview of this in the '60s, when I was less than thirty myself. Suddenly, for no apparent reason, while teaching a college class, I knew: these young women were born a year or more after Hiroshima. The ground between us crumbled, making a trench I'd seen only from the other side. For the first time I felt myself in other people's ice age, partly dead, as my parents had been partly dead to me because they had one foot in HISTORY—World War I, horses and carriages, Teddy Roosevelt. I was distorted, the 1940s were distorted. And not only I, but the atrocities of Hiroshima and Auschwitz were suddenly made less significant.

It's dangerous, and it's not just "natural," this separation of generations. It serves patriarchy to wipe out the past as quickly as possible or to make sure the scraps that remain seem irrelevant to today. Maybe there never really were Amazons or witch-burnings, maybe six million Jews did not really die. Or: maybe it's true that men who came from England to this continent slaughtered peaceful peoples and seized their land, maybe it's true they dragged women and men from Africa to work under the lash—but all of that is very long ago. Surely the Indians should be assimilated by now, not stirring up hard feelings; surely Black people should not still be expecting reparations for that ancient mistake.

The voice that quickly covers the path we have just taken becomes one with the voice that hustles us on towards the newest. Don't live in the past, it says. Don't romanticize the primitive. What counts is progress, and look how far we've come. Would you want to live way back then in a world without automobiles? without airplanes? without television? frozen foods? nuclear energy? cellular phones? Star Wars? Would you want to wear a mini-skirt when maxi-skirts are the latest? Whatever is now is good, and obviously getting better—look, when you were a kid, there were no VCRs.

And as the old people of each generation take measure of what they've seen in their lifetimes, they are labelled sentimental, tiresome. So if we too remember when the water was drinkable, or the fish were alive in Santa Monica Bay, or the sky over the ocean was blue not brown, or the soil was free of DDT and PCBs, we'd best keep quiet or we'll sound like one of those old fogies who go on about the "good old days."

I've lived more than half a century now, and nobody can tell me that's a long time. Sometimes when I wander through the desert and pick up rosy pottery shards, or stop to look at the smooth bowl of a mortero or to finger the stones of a sleeping circle, I feel I am walking through the rubble of a recently destroyed town, a little Beirut, a bombed Salvadorian village. And I am.

The Inyakiipaa Indians lived on this land until the mid-1950s. Here's another case of how the victor controls the language. I can't say the Indians *owned* the land, since they believe no one should or could *own* land. But I also can't say that the Indians *didn't own* this land, since in Anglo dialect that implies they had no rights to stay here. What happened here on the Anza-Borrego must not really have happened, since there is no language to explain it.

In the early '50s, Anglos would come to pitch tents on the desert and bathe in these springs for free, here where the Indians lived. Down the road past where Vi's store now stands was a trading post. Eva tells me about Dora who was born here and stayed here with her daughter after the county took over the springs—they permitted her to rent a small space on the land where her people lived for centuries. But in the 1970s a new Head Ranger began to make up lots of rules; one of them was that Dora couldn't keep her tiny refrigerator in the shed on her site, and there wasn't room for it inside her trailer. So Dora had to leave. Her parents didn't need a fridge because they summered up in the Lagunas, but then they didn't need to pay rent wherever they travelled, either. She moved to Warner Springs reservation, but from time to time she still comes back to look around, and stops by to visit with Eva. She's 100 now.

Barbara and I are standing on a street corner in Laguna Beach, trying to decide where to have lunch. A car drives by, and a white man in his late twenties with a dark moustache leans his head far out of the window to scream at us. "Go to hell, dykes!" The cry lingers on the street after he has passed.

We look at each other to make sure we heard right. We weren't touching each other. We are dressed as we usually are on the desert or in the city—pants from Sears, a simple woman's shirt, sneakers.

Then we begin to laugh—elated, triumphant laughter. Just walking down the street, a white-haired woman with a grey-haired woman, talking about lunch—still they know who we are. And they know our power! They know we are a threat!

The Code

Muriel, Margaret and Glinda drove out from San Diego and stopped by for a few hours. It's hard to explain to friends from San Diego or Boston what this community of permittees is like, how we can be so independent of each other and yet so linked. We are people who didn't choose each other. We come from very different classes, politics, religions. Still, like most communities, we've a sense of belonging. We talk about *them* and *us*, though less belligerently than most.

"It's getting hot now, but *we* don't mind, do we?"

"My family can't understand how I can live out here. *They* don't think the desert is beautiful at all. *They* don't understand what I see in it. *They* can't imagine living without a telephone."

The reality of the heat and what *we* know as the

fiction of the desert's barrenness are all that preserves this place from *them. They* would come in with their condominiums and shopping malls and three combustion engines to a family if *they* were not afraid of heat and isolation, if *they* loved this place as *we* do.

We are connected by that common love. We are connected—curiously—by our willingness to engage with solitude. And we are connected because our choice to live here, together with the fact that we are no longer young or part of the work force, makes us odd and irrelevant to the rest of the world.

We have a code, unspoken, essential. I suspect every community has its own code, only ours is sharper, as everything is on the desert. *Don't borrow anything that might break or need replacing*—a flashlight, an aspirin tablet. We live far from stores, and each of us has pared her life down to what is for her the necessary core. *Don't ask for favors.* Vivian and Marge are in wheelchairs; Lucille, Helen and Kathryn walk with pain; Jake has difficulty breathing; Lilla cares for a husband who's been frail all his life since an auto crash, and so on. We don't exaggerate need. Partly this is the world of the disabled for whom challenge isn't exotic and for whom freedom from pain is known as a blessing rather than a right. Partly, to be less than stalwart would drain a community that can't afford such luxury.

We are unsolicitous of each other and it is our way of loving. We send each other desert messages. You are strong enough to endure. We know you can do it.

This is not the code we were socialized by in childhood. In the mainstream, we learned that a man's value lies in his accomplishments, a woman's in meeting needs. So in our hunger to be valued, we often cultivate dependencies. At times in my life I have urgently needed neediness. Has it taken the other desert women years of living, too, to discover the lesson of wildness: that our value rests in our being, not for barter?

Yet we help each other in tiny ways that make living here possible. Picking up mail for someone who's unable to walk or drive the quarter mile to her rural mailbox beyond the store, volunteering to shop for somebody's groceries if she is absolutely unable to get to town.

The code also says, *Don't ask personal questions.* A personal question is: Did you have a good time in town? Have you heard from your sister lately? If I want to tell you about my trip to town or my sister, I am free to do so, and you may then ask me a few questions until I show some signs of closure. This might make a fine rule for families or for any other unchosen community as well. We are too different from each other, too close, too exposed to one another, encircled as we are by miles of desert, to bear a casual intrusiveness that presumes an intimacy we couldn't live out. Our intimacy is not around private griefs or joys or anxieties but around survival and solitude and a shared love of the land.

So it follows, of course, that the code also says, *Don't talk politics.* There is one exception—one area we can at least touch on safely because we all agree:

67

there should be a national health program, more rights for the disabled, and most doctors are ignorant and dangerous.

Stop Me
If I've Told You

After almost nineteen years here, Eva has taken into her cells the non-linear rhythms of the desert. When we're out walking, she may tell me something—"I hope a lot of campers come for the weekend. It's good for the store." Maybe she'll repeat herself fifteen minutes later in a slightly different form or even use the same words. She's perfectly aware of the repetition and at ease with it. I find myself speaking in the same ways, especially when Barbara's been gone for a week.

I realize how, without noticing it, most of us keep a constant record of what we've said to different people. Sometimes we slip up and repeat ourselves, though usually not in the space of a few hours. We signal our embarrassment about possible repetitions, saying, "Stop me if I've told you . . . " or "Did I tell you that . . . " or "As I said before . . . ." Goddess forbid we should say something more than once!

In fact, there's nothing wrong with repetition, it's just a different song. It's closer to poetry, to the life of our bodies, to the pulse of the seasons. Indian thought and speech don't strive to follow on a track like a railroad engine.

If the goal of conversation is to achieve something hard-nosed, specific—draft a proposal, learn as many new things as possible—repetition is inefficient. But when life is simpler, without the self-conscious bustle from one idea to the next, conversation doesn't cease to be valued. Sometimes we want to share, for instance, memories or fears with someone because the sharing itself makes memory more meaningful or eases a fear. Then repetition can be almost erotic in its lilt.

When we spend a lot of time alone, we may speak our hoarded thoughts with special intensity—so the listener wants to say "take it easy"—or we may be looking for that deep peace of a speech that exists primarily to affirm connection. Eva knows I've heard many times the story of how she and Rosie used to look for arrowheads on their long walks through the desert. But if we can connect the pleasure of our walking together with the pleasure of her memories of Rosie, that creates a new pleasure. Why should she restrict either of us to one dose of such pleasure?

The desert women are much alone, though we may meet at mailtime or on evening walks. But it's the married women, who come with their husbands for a few months to give the desert a try, whose speech

70

reveals the pain of loneliness. Their words spill out when we meet, padded accounts of the inconsequential, hidden appeals for something unnamed— tenderness, attention, passion? They themselves don't know what. Barbara and I laugh sometimes— "You can always spot a married woman because she can't stop talking"—but I know their urgency. They've never, all their lives, had the chance to find intimacy with themselves. Rather, they've lived, as I once did, in a parody of intimacy, that promises closeness and attention but doesn't deliver. Now they find themselves in a trailer with that stranger they married, no job or telephone or coffee with neighborhood women to relieve the stored-up pressures. Their speech says, "Listen to me, please do!" but the words are still monitored.

Those who come with such hunger rarely stay long. Their need is not fed on the desert, and they find reasons to leave. Meanwhile we've learned not to engage them in conversation.

When Barbara is atop the trailer roof, plugging a leak, she's fair game for a shouted "What are you doing?" That's only the opener for what follows: "You shouldn't be up there." And then the stream pours upward, no need for a ladder, while Barbara keeps on patching to stay ahead of the noonday sun. Nothing she says could meet the force of such longing, and it might take a lifetime to explain what she is doing.

Sometimes I think how, in the world out there, both those love-hungry monologues and Eva's pleasurable repetitions are seen as the mark of old women who are probably halfway senile. But then I remember that old women are marked before they even begin to speak. A 30-year-old woman who says, "When I was a child . . . " inspires interest; when an old woman says it, the world closes its ears.

I invented an experiment that's useful for gauging our ageism. You watch a talk show on TV or go to a political meeting, and listen to how people talk. Then picture them as old women. That young woman who speaks intensely or claims her space to explain something, who a moment ago seemed simply passionate or involved, may surprise you by turning to caricature—embarrassing, boring, intolerable.

Wild Beasts and Postage Stamps

Walking through the lower campground at twilight on a fall evening, I'm getting nostalgic as usual looking at the spare, snug little tents and the camping trailers with their windows zipped against the chill. A man is standing outside against the light from one of the camper doors. I see him startle, then brace himself and call urgently behind him: "Betsy, don't come out! A coyote has wandered into camp!" He's looking down on the ground for a stone.

I glance ahead to the other side of the road and see her, picking her way across the white rock, turned on by the promise of hamburger scraps, a spare hot dog roll.

Quickly I call out, "She won't hurt you! They never bother anybody." I hope Betsy has heard me.

Any time we sit out in the evening, one or more

coyotes will walk by. They move with great presence, a solid kind of grace, and we watch their coats change from silky full to sparse with the seasons. Occasionally a young one will come onto our site, just a few yards from our beach chairs. In the spring, the little rabbits jump over each other's backs near our feet. A kitfox stared at me once from the canyon wall with quiet interest while I was walking alone.

Often Barbara and I laugh at the myth of Man the Defender, who from the dawn of history has protected helpless Betsys from the vicious wild beasts. It's a small step from that fantasy of danger to the takeover of Grenada. We are so obviously not the coyote's or the bobcat's prey, or at least not until our spreading city asphalt traps them in narrow canyons without enough food. Our automobiles kill thousands of animals large and small on desert roads, to say nothing of our guns. Last month, a local rancher was showing off thirty coyote pelts. A week later, Vi found Big Red, the lame coyote who lived in our park for years, smashed by a car on the side of the road.

Much of desert talk is about the animals. The raccoon with the wounded foot I saw catching the drip from a faucet. Boots spotted three different quail families this week, one with twenty-four newly feathered little ones. The finch's nest with five tiny white eggs, wreathed with spring flowers on a post under the mailboxes—will it be disturbed when Wally the mailman slams the metal doors to the boxes? Will the bobcat come back this year and eat the rabbits and the nervy little shawl squirrels?

Every now and then field mice find a way into the trailer, scuttling through the cupboards after dark. But Eva's small cage and a splash of peanut butter catch them. After hearing the snap of the door, we carry them outside and lift the screen. They sit immobilized by freedom for a minute, before rushing into the bushes.

In late spring we're careful about walking through rocky canyons because of the rattlesnakes, but even they will give more warning than a gun and as much as an automobile. And the only people they've bitten in this county in ten years were "children" (little boys?) or "people" (men?) who'd been drinking, which sounds like self-defense in my court.

Each year in June, counters arrive at Carrizo Canyon and Borrego to count the bighorn sheep. The sheep used to come down in summer from the mountains in large herds to the desert watering spots. There are few of them now, and people who have lived here for decades have never seen one. Not so many years ago, a man named Gary Swanson had an operation going in Carrizo: he and several hired men would shoot the sheep to sell the mounted heads. He made $40,000 a year just on the bighorns. They fined him but he came back; they fined him again but he came back; it went on like that for years until the fines and the hassles made it less worthwhile, and he moved on to Arizona.

Barbara and I are on the mailing list for catalogues like Orvis and Eddie Bauer, and we sometimes comment on how it's the men whose pleasure comes from slaughtering ducks who like to have sentimental paintings of ducks hanging on their walls or printed on their mugs, cigarette lighters or doormats.

Well, Vi's a stamp collector so she happened to notice. When the stamp of the bighorn sheep was issued, she noticed that the name of the artist was Gary Swanson.

When we first came west, I went to a workshop in San Francisco where the leader gave the results of the first questionnaire sent to old lesbians. One question was: how do you like to spend your time? And the answer, overwhelmingly, was gardening. I winced. I saw a hundred old dykes mindlessly training roses instead of organizing to end ageism. And gardening sounded awfully classist, as I forgot how many inner city roses I'd seen, or Alice Walker's descriptions of her mother's garden.

I see it differently now. I see women in male-designed cities as displaced persons, like Palestinians or Jews before Israel, with a huge homesickness that builds for our grounding in nature. The old women who garden, the lesbians who "go back to the land," Barbara and I on the desert, are making an essential reconnection. It can mean privilege, it can mean isolation from political realities, a merely 'personal solution,' but it doesn't have to. It can mean knowledge brought back to the cities. Knowledge that says: our right to live with nature is as basic as our right to sexuality.

The desert lets me feel how flimsy my life was in cities, in suburbs. When I lived in the suburbs, we kept trees and flowers and shrubs like household pets, training them to fit our whims. Even driving to the country was like a trip to the zoo—here and there that glimpse of what she might have been left wild, but hard to shake the notion that she existed mostly to provide us with that weekend dose of beauty. In the cities, I and everybody else ignored her most of the day. When I worked at Digital, I had to stand up from my desk to see a thin slice of sky. It could rain or snow without my knowing. None of us, blinking into our word processors, found that especially odd.

Now it seems to me that I was never meant to live any piece of my day forgetting my context in the natural world. I don't mean just a squirrel in the park, daffodils in front of a florist, a patch of sun during lunch break. I mean the knowledge each evening of whether the moon will rise through that notch in the mountains or over the flat rim of horizon to the north, and knowing whether it will rise tonight as a C or an O. I mean a context that clearly instructs me that I was made to walk on dirt or sand, not asphalt, that the snow doesn't fall for the skiers, that the daffodils grow for themselves and the bees, not for my picking, that the animals are not here as my servants, my enemies, or even my companions.

This is the first place I have lived year-round where I am continually informed that I belong on earth no more and no less than any other species. Sometimes I tune out that message, but I have enough reminders so that it is sweetness, clarity, relief. Nature

in her wildness is not a luxury, but a political neces-
sity, since she sets out the terms of a sane society.

I love living with less of that false power I had in
cities. I never trusted it, especially as a woman power-
less in so many ways. If you throw out the hierarchy of
Adam-over-Eve, you're bound to be suspicious of
other dominion-overs.

In late November, Barbara and I have the flu, a sullen,
unforgiving flu. I'm sitting at my work table, pretending to write a letter. The grey skies have washed the
color from the desert and so I quickly spot the reddish
coat of the dog wandering down through the creosote
bushes. Dogs aren't allowed in the park, which is an
animal preserve. She is large and looks as thin as
Nancy Reagan on election night, but all starvation
isn't the same. She must have travelled for some time
after somebody let her loose and lost her, or let her
loose and drove away. Quickly she's the talk of the
camp, mainly of the rangers who say she's wild and
certainly vicious and might bite a camper if she's not
caught soon. For four days they stand searching the
desert with binoculars and a few times try chasing her.
"She was seen in Squaw Canyon yesterday afternoon," "She was on the path to the Moonlight Trail
this morning," is the news at the mailbox.

Late one afternoon, the green ranger's truck
backs into the lot of our neighbor, Roy, and the two
rangers in the truck chat with him for a minute. He
nods, goes into his little trailer and comes out with a
rifle. Twenty-four feet of living space, and he's found

room for a rifle. We don't even have a full-sized broom. As Roy passes the rifle to Mike, they laugh. I don't hear the words that go with the laugh, but there it is. Barbara, who worked for years in a kennel, pulls herself off the bed and grabs a piece of cheese from the refrigerator. She roams the desert awhile, but it's getting too dark to see. Somewhere the red dog is out there trying to be a coyote, to find a rabbit or a field mouse, and tomorrow morning the guys will be out looking for her again, this time with their firepower.

At breakfast time, we're talking about it. Down the road comes Boots' grey cropped head and string-bean body. She's holding one end of a slack rope, and ambling beside her is the red dog, looking relieved and contented as if she had good memories of walks on a lead. Barbara and I whoop together, and that afternoon I put a ribbon on Boots' trailer door that reads "Brains Not Bullets."

Shoot to Destroy
and Other Ways of
Raising Children

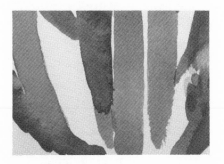

From an Atari game in an ice cream store/video parlor in Borrego Springs:

Shoot to destroy advancing creatures for points.

Collisions with any creature will destroy you.

In a two player game, players alternate until his supply of lives is exhausted.

Hold fire button down for repetitive fire.

In Thrifty's in San Diego, I hear a piercing boy's voice from the next aisle: "Look at the guns, Mommy! I want one of the guns." Of course they're not selling rifles in Thrifty's yet, he means a "toy." I look up to see Mommy, a middle-class white woman, rush around the corner. I hear her whispering, and I know the words. I've been a mother, forbidding guns, organizing protests of toy stores, but always wondering whether my son's rat-a-tat with a stick was an improvement. Just a few years later he was registering proudly for the draft.

In several minutes, we're all at the check-out counter together. Mommy is behind me, with no gun in her carriage, and a blond restless eight-year-old at her side. I catch her eye and try to send her knowledge across generations.

"He's eight years old and he already has the message that someday he'll shoot somebody."

Her face collapses with pain and guilt. I've become her own voice, now from outside.

"I've *told* him he can't have guns. I hate them. It's all he can talk about."

You think it's your fault and it's not, that's what I was trying to tell you, I want to say, but it's my turn at check-out.

Driving through the dark back to the desert, I think of the should-have-said. It wouldn't have made her feel better, but it's the truth. *If in eight years we haven't been able to teach our sons that guns are evil, why do we dream that we can teach them anything?* It's so hard for women to confront the fact that we are not raising our children. We are baby-sitter, cook, maid, nurse, governess for children, but they learn "our" values only when "our" values fit with the patriarchy's. Women's dream that we can change the world by changing our children—that our children will be better—makes it easy to use us, easy to tame and co-opt the longing we have to create a different world.

Every February, a bit north of El Centro in the little town of Holtville, they hold an air show. Barbara and I stayed one night in a motel cabin in Holtville when we first drove across the country to come here. The sidewalks were sunbaked mud and the wind from the desert blew clouds of dust across the streets. But for three days in February, the Combat Heritage Foundation presents a spectacle in Holtville: "War in Europe—World War II." The pamphlet we picked up in El Centro promises FUN ENTERTAINMENT NOSTALGIA PRIDE. For just $12.00 ($3.00 for a child), you are invited to watch two hours of simulated air and ground battles. "Come early for good parking spot. Bring your own folding chairs. Booths featuring wide variety of food and beverages."

When I was a child, a teacher told our class that the moral progress of Mankind was slow but steady, and we could measure it because in 18th-century England, people used to bring their lunches and families and go to watch hangings.

We drive to Solana Beach to have dinner at Kate and Joyce's, with ten other women who have come together to meet Sonia Johnson and her partner Susan. We've met the other women, though we don't know them well.

After dinner, we're sitting around talking about our visions for the world we'd like to live in. I'm talking about the numbers of people who would be in my best

world, and how the present population is so stagger-
ing because through history women have had almost
no choice about whether or when we will have sexual
intercourse, whether or not we will bear children.
Even when women thought we were choosing (when
we weren't raped, coerced, denied access to birth
control), our choices have often been made from a
poverty of options.

"Why don't we just go around the room," says
Lori, "and see—just in this group—how many children would be here if there hadn't been pressures on
us to become mothers?"

So we do, consciousness-raising style, each
woman talking out of a private painful space, then
listening as each space opens out to meet the spaces
of the other women, until a lighter airier place is
created where we can see more and breathe more
easily.

Among the twelve of us we have doubled our
numbers, bearing twenty-two children. But if we had
had the support we have today, we would have borne
seven. Sally, the mother of two of these, says: "I'm glad
I had my children, but I can't even imagine whether
I'd have been a mother if from my earliest childhood
there had been other choices. I was told from infancy
that this was what I was going to do, so it's what I did."

There goes three-quarters of the world's
population.

Our youngest child is twelve, we've had a chance
to live through a lot of mothering, and we are awed by
the pain and the enormity of it. Even two women who
say they would help run the child care spaces in a

84

woman's world know that the exclusivity of the mother-bond, the measureless responsibility for the life of another that is supposed to end only with death, is harmful to both. Many of us say the unspeakable— that even when we love our children deeply, we find the relationship of mother and child in patriarchy to be so impossible, so loaded with lies and roles and guilt, that if we could, we would free ourselves of it.

I swallow my fear and speak for the first time openly, in a group, of my refusal to be mired in that impossibility, how I live across the country from my daughter, see her rarely, talk to her occasionally, write from time to time. I speak of how she is exactly the kind of young woman I would love to know if she were not my daughter, and how it grieves and maddens me that *because* she is my daughter I can't know her, she can't know me. Not because of distance, not because I am a lesbian, but *because* she is my daughter.

. . . And Other Ways of Killing

I'm standing at the sink washing the lunch dishes. It's April and the wind has been fierce for the past five days; most of the weekend campers have gone home disappointed. Through the window I see two men standing by the side of the road for a long time, but my glasses aren't on and I figure they are last campers. I don't know they are gathering courage to come to my open door. Barbara's in Connecticut giving a talk. Helen and Roy who live in this section of the camp are gone for the weekend, and mine's the only open door.

When they come near, they are each holding two large plastic water bottles and they tap the bottles. They are Mexicans, who have walked fifty miles or more from the border across the desert.

"De l'agua?" I ask and they nod.

I take two bottles—how long have they been empty?—fill them at my tap, hand them back, fill two more. I try to remember the word for store.

"Allí hay una bodega," I say, pointing down the desert. They frown. I didn't get it right.

"La policía?" one man asks.

"No, no policía. Allí está una *tienda* y un teléfono."

They nod. "Gracias," one man says. "De nada," I say. They head down towards the store. None of us has smiled once. Both men are, like myself, in their fifties. I can still feel the weight of those gallon jugs on my wrist.

Sometimes women make the trip. Three sisters—Isadora Olivares-Ortiz, 35, Audelia Olivares-Ortiz de Martinez, 25, and Balbina Olivares-Ortiz de Pacheco, 30—were found dead in September of dehydration. They were part of a group of a dozen sisters, brothers, cousins and friends who crossed the border together, travelling up from Guanajuato. They had heard of the dream but not the details, apparently, since they had brought just five gallons of water and one of the women was wearing high heels. It was 112°, and one of the survivors told the sheriff how in the intense heat they were forced to drink their own urine.

But usually the women wait, in shanties without plumbing, hoping for news and a little money against the hunger, trying to make it alone with their children.

It's mostly men you see walking in the heat of the morning along the highway, a few clothes and a bottle of water in a rucksack on their backs. Sometimes at night a flashlight gleams on the desert or we hear someone filling a water jug at our hose. Sometimes we find a blanket, a few empty soda pop cans and an empty bag of tortilla chips under a creosote bush. It is the Underground Railroad of the '80s. By word of mouth they know where to find water or shade trees (few places indeed), where the store is with its telephone to call the coyotes whom they'll pay to take them by car to Los Angeles.

If they were escaping from East to West Germany they'd be heroes, walking through the river and then fifty miles under the uncompromising sun for the chance of what we call "a better life." Instead they are hunted, persistently but randomly, since the name of the game is to let enough through to become workers below the minimum wage for the agri-businesses and an intimidated labor force for factories. A few may find odd jobs, a bit of gardening here, some hauling there. The rounding up of Mexicans is rather like the rounding up of prostitutes, a question of jockeying the numbers of service providers, keeping them poor and anxious without eliminating the service. Some are El Salvadorians or Guatemalans, of course—political refugees by any definition—who already have made the long trek through Mexico, and they have the most to fear. Unlike the Mexicans who are driven back to the border, they are most likely to find themselves in the El Centro detention camp fifty miles from here, awaiting deportation to the dangers they escaped. In the detention camp they are made to stand in the courtyard between 6:00 A.M. and 6:00 P.M. in heat that's sometimes 130°. Before they cross the border, they learn a few phrases of Mexican slang, try to pick up the Mexican lilt, so they can pass for illegal Mexicans.

I felt no fear today, out of calling range of neighbors, when the two men came to my door, and the absence of fear feels strange and a great relief, such as I feel walking at night in San Francisco's Castro district. These men have little in common with the gay men of San Francisco, but like gay men, they have other fish to fry.

It's almost unheard of for them to steal, rape, murder. Anyone who walks fifty miles through the desert does so for a larger hope, not to be arrested for a crime that brings only momentary relief to hunger or rage.

When I go to Los Angeles for the Jobs, Peace and Freedom demo, I get up at 4:00 A.M. to drive eighty miles to Carlsbad to catch one of two schoolbuses filled with San Diegans. The desert's an awkward place for an activist.

I've never been in L.A. before, just driven through holding my nose, and I like it better than I'd thought now that I'm part of the stream of people marching from Olympic to City Hall Plaza. Unlike so many Saturday demos where I've walked past empty office buildings shouting only to other marchers, this time the streets are crowded with faces, Black, Asian, Latino, turned to watch us. I long to know what they make of us, mostly white Anglos, Jews, faggots and dykes.

Sharon got there early to find me and we're marching with the multi-colored, multi-issued signs of the New Jewish Agenda. Deciding where to march was like perusing a buffet. Would we choose to end nuclear war or the war in Central America? Would we stop supporting apartheid and racism or the regime of Marcos, the deportation of Mexicans or uranium mining on Indian reservations? Or would we prefer to stop terrorism against women's health clinics (last week the L.A. clinic burned down)?

The night before, in our desert trailer, I stared down at my blank posterboard for ten minutes, feeling crazier by the minute. You now have two lines in which to give your message to the world. I finally shrugged, took my magic marker and wrote, "$$ for Life, Not $$ for Death." Like the New Jewish Agenda, it seemed inclusive enough.

It is my first march with heterosexual men in many years—or at least on Jesse Jackson's march to the border last summer, the gay section was large enough to insulate me. It's a shock to find myself again with straight male monitors. A seven-foot guy with a voice that could break glass is leading the chants in our area, and I remember the sweet relief of my first women's march, when I could give the responses to a woman's voice, and thought my life was changed forever. It was. But here I am, echoing this guy I'm looking up to.

At the plaza, the multitude of inhumanities splash down the steps onto the crowd from the speakers' microphone. We are drowning, though it feels sane-making for 5000 people to be testifying to those horrors and making the connections. That's the best part of the march.

But although everybody gets his or her say and even "sexual preference" is given a nod, I'm acutely aware that "sexism" is in a back seat, a fairly minor agenda item, barely rescued from the petty bourgeois by last week's bombing of the women's health clinic. How is it that, when the executives of these evils are men, and more than half of the world's population are women—who live in the crossfire of generalized male violence but are the direct targets of woman-hating besides—how is it that "imperialism" has so much more the ring, in this plaza, of explaining everything? I think of Robin Morgan, after a lecture in the early '70s, responding to the inevitable question, "Are you sure that if women ran the world it would be any better?" She said she thought it would be, but that if she were backed to the wall, she would just say that in all of recorded history it had never been tried, and at the very least it was our *turn*. But somehow it never is our turn and it seems the last idea on anybody's mind right now.

On our evening walk, we stop at the ranger station to chat with Mike, the head ranger. We've heard he's leaving in a few months.

"It's an office job in Santee," he says, proud of his promotion. "I'll be in charge of maintenance—they plan to construct more parks."

"They'll need a lot for all the people," says Boots.

"That's right," I add. "And if they don't stop having babies, in ten years there'll be a shopping mall in Shelter Valley."

A blond young man comes up to the booth to speak to Mike; his toddler is testing out her new steps along the walk. He's heard me. I turn to him and say: "*She's* great, but it's time to stop."

He looks at me aghast, and of course I think he doesn't want me monitoring his conceptions. Then I glance at the kid's sweatshirt, which says "Padres," and I realize she's a he.

But I mean it, it can't go on. We are killing ourselves and the rest of the world with these births. Not Third World births, whatever they try to tell us, American births. It's we, a tiny six percent of the world's population, who use up half of the raw materials that the world consumes every year.

Most of the radical or liberal movements for change imply a world in which everybody would live in families and have, more or less, an American standard of living. Supposedly the only obstacles to that dream are the expensive arms race and the refusal of powerful nations to share the wealth. But the dream itself is a lie, and because we suspect it's a lie, I think we are less ready to face what in fact we can do. We can: feed everyone on this planet by making that a priority. But we need to give up our romance with what Winona LaDuke, an Ojibwa economist, calls our "technoculture"—plastic wrap, cans, beef cattle, food processors, computers, deodorants and the armies of consumers needed to fuel those industries.

I saw a TV documentary once on people who live in the Amazon jungles. I suspect life wasn't very different for the Indians here on this desert. If they needed to cut down a tree, they first would ask pardon from the tree's spirit, explaining exactly what it would be used for and why they needed it so much. If the chairman of the Brazilian cattle industry followed that rule, would the trees be disappearing, and with them the earth's ozone?

And I imagine it could be like this: Each woman who was thinking of having a child would talk to the earth. She might assure it that she is aware that its human numbers double every forty years, plundering its plants and minerals, driving out its animals and birds. She would give a calculation of how many tons of oil, copper, aluminum, plastic, how many toxic chemicals that child would use and discard in a lifetime. How many trees and animals, how much water. Then she might speak to convince the earth why her own need was so immense to bear a child, rather than join in caring for children who are already here and needing.

When *Gay Community News* appears in our mailbox, I open it to see a picture of two lesbians announcing the birth of a bouncing boy. I am glad that lesbians can afffirm our right to bear children, for it's been hard won. But I'm saddened and exasperated, too, that it's the right we've chosen to affirm at this moment on earth.

For, in our essence, the lesbian challenges the proposition that family is the only way to organize society, the Indian challenges the proposition that technology means progress. These are the gifts of our being, the secrets we embody for surviving in the 21st century, and we assimilate not only at our own peril but at the world's.

On those mornings when I open the *San Diego Union,* I catch glimpses that begin to tell me where I live in today's history, today's geography. I read that Imperial County, twenty miles east of here, has been recommended as a site for the dumping of radioactive wastes—it is, after all, just desert. I learn that arsine, a highly toxic form of arsenic, used in the manufacture of computer chips, is produced in La Mesa, a suburb of San Diego, and trucks carry it day and night along Route 8, thirty miles east of here, though any spill would be deadly. To the south, in the Laguna Mountains, the Campo Indian Reservation was chosen for a toxic waste "storage facility" by the company that used to manufacture PCBs—the Lieutenant Governor stopped it, but only because it was an out-of-state firm. Just past Julian, the tiny town of Santa Isabel can't drink their own well water because of leaks from gasoline storage tanks.

This is the hometown news that all Americans take in for breakfast. Nothing special here, only that this is Americans' wildness, a remote and relatively untouched area with no history of heavy industry, no nearby nuclear power plant, no uranium mines, no history of nuclear bomb testing as in Nevada or New Mexico. Yet the threats aren't just recent, even here.

In spring, we drive out to a sandy hillside over-looking Carrizo Wash. We wander along the wash, looking up at the bank swarming with purple lupine and monkey flowers, creamy and pink primroses, yellow poppies, pale ghost flowers, and rising above them, the green and crimson ocotillo and great clumps of golden brittle bush. Down below we search for the white spectacle flower with its giddying fragrance, and the lavender globe of the rare fivespot. Our desert handbook says that in this ten-mile area more varieties of flowers bloom than any place on the desert. But in the same handbook, I learn that just five miles further down the wash is the Carrizo Impact Area, 27,000 acres closed off from the world. This land was used for bombing practice in World War II, and despite intense efforts to remove the live shells, they haven't been able to make it safe for people or animals, not in forty years.

These past few months, there's been a change. Half a mile away across the desert is an airstrip, built by the county years ago as an odd fringe benefit for a ranger who had his own plane. We'd almost forgotten it was there. But now every Friday night at seven o'clock, two helicopters appear on the field for an hour, circling and landing, circling and landing. Nobody knows who they are, but here where the sound of a bee in the mesquite outside the bathroom window can wake us in the morning, the buzzing roar of their engines resounds against the mountains, and we feel we are inside a dentist's drill.

When they first came, we would pace and peer like caged animals, trying to play poker but finding ourselves pulled to the windows. As if our looking could stop them, when it's just what they would like best.

One night, I can't stand the helplessness any longer and charge off in the Datsun. I head down to the airstrip where the guys are circling. Barbara's stayed to watch through her binoculars.

Every woman knows this anger—it's peculiarly female. It is the fury of violation, fury at a male world that always, anywhere, believes it has a right to invade our space—that, in fact, does have that right. It's the rage of choosing to refuse that victimization, while you know that your refusal invites worse victimization. What am I doing on a deserted airstrip in the desert night?

Barbara didn't say "Go," she didn't say "Don't go," but I knew she wanted to say both, because I've been in a place where I wanted to say both to her.

I drive onto the airstrip and park there, with my doors locked, my headlights on, my window open just enough to talk through but not enough for a hand or a gun. I don't know what will happen—I'm too mad to care. I figure they'll either leave, or more likely, come over and chew me out for parking there, in which case I'll chew them out and find out who they are. Instead, they start to buzz me, zooming like thunder through the darkness down over the roof of the Datsun over and over and over again. I start up the motor and head home, defeated, furious.

Not long afterwards, little twin-engines start to appear on weekends, practicing maneuvers, roaring in and out all day.

I talk to Mike, the head ranger. He nods and shrugs. "Better buy earplugs. The airfield's on the Palomar map now. The county wanted to put in hangars and lights. I talked them out of that one, that's as far as I could go."

Barbara's in town for the week, and I face my anger alone. I scrape together shreds of my lost faith in democracy and decide to organize a petition. After all, this is an animal preserve, the campers are here to enjoy the silence, the permittees are here for medical reasons—oh, I know, but at least we could feel we'd done something, taken a stand. For as different as we are, a shared love of this place binds us together— male and female, lesbian and straight, Christian and Jew, Falwell follower and radical feminist. I start to go round: "I wanted to talk to you because you're a real desert lover."

In half an hour I'm home. I've found out that in our tiny community four men are ex-military pilots. The roar of airplanes is music, reminding them of their finest hours.

It's a morning in May, and I'm driving out early to Borrego. I can't figure it out—there's a sort of haze against the mountains and the sky lacks authority. One of the sure things on the desert is the definition of rock and shrub, every outline of the natural world standing sharp and brazen. After three years, I still exclaim to Barbara almost daily about the sky, a blue you could fall into.

But today's different, and after twenty-five minutes, I turn the sharp bend down into Shelter Valley and see it. Seeping between the mountains from the other side of Julian, it's thick enough to be smoke except for the giveaway pink. In three years, I've never seen the like of it.

So we've lost. We came so far and risked a lot, and we thought we'd won just a toehold, a little patch of sanity that might last fifteen or twenty years if there wasn't a nuclear war first. And in barely three years we lost it.

I remember Jake saying, "San Diego is a gas chamber."

I want to scream and wail and I want someone to scream with me. To say I am not crazy, not "overreacting."

And what is Jake to do, who managed, in the '40s, not to die in a gas chamber?

When I get to Borrego, and buy my faucet and bread and salsa, I feel like the lesbian whose lover has been raped, who must go to work and never say anything.

Were Barbara and I like survivalists, then, dreaming we could hole up in some corner and not share the planet's collapse? Not really.

Only at times it seemed if the Anza-Borrego could stay clear, there might still be hope that the dirty air, water, soil of the rest of the world could be reversed. At least she'd be there to tell us what was possible.

That night when I come home, the air is thick against Whale Mountain. "I hate to say anything about it today," I say softly to Barbara, "when you're in the middle of working, but it's so much on my mind."

Her blue eyes blaze at me. "I know. I saw it this morning, and I've been feeling it all day. I couldn't decide whether to say anything."

As though not to say would keep our lost world real for the other a few days, a few weeks longer.

Barbara and I rage plenty about rape, murder, wars. But for some reason the violation of this place we love like a third lover mutes us. Maybe we think if we began to howl, to weep or rage, there'd be no end.

Sometime in the next few days we go to El Centro for groceries. On the return trip which we always savor, I stop the car at the top of Sweeney Pass, only fifteen miles from home. The drama of the rosy bad-lands, the crisp sweep of desert circled with sensuous mountains, the stunning sky—it's hardly to be recognized. Directly above I can see the sky still boldly blue, so it's not a cloudy day, but ahead and below somebody's chalky hand has willfully, arrogantly smeared and defaced. Even before belief hardens, we know that in this moment the terms of our life have changed.

The New Order

The word is that the new Head Ranger will be a woman, for the first time in the history of the park. The male rangers are furious.

Last spring these men laughed when they told us they'd be gone for the afternoon to attend a county-wide workshop on sexual harassment. I suspect there was a case, too big to ignore, and that's why they're suddenly hiring women supervisors.

Only Ernie, a former ranger who at 83 is now a volunteer in exchange for his rent, says to me: "I won't mind. I don't think people ought to be judged ahead of time." But then Ernie knows that the younger rangers don't listen to him.

At the pool, Vivian, Eva and I discuss the change. Vivian tells us that one of the rangers is quitting.

"He told the guys, 'If she gets it, put my name in

the hat—I'm clearing out.' And sure enough he's leaving come July."

Eva stretches out her legs and gives her toes a loving smile. "The park will still run."

I tell them Barbara's comment: Reneene is in an impossible position. If she doesn't follow the book to the letter, they'll call her lenient. If she does, they'll say she's rigid and demanding. She can't win.

Vivian scowls at the sun. "I know what she's up against. I was a businesswoman." After her husband walked out on her, she ran a tiny grocery store in Imperial Beach. She had a garden out back, and when customers would say, "No parsley today?" she'd go out and snip them a bunch. She hurt her back in 1969 and is still trying to get disability. Meanwhile, she makes yarn dolls and mobiles from beer cans to sell at the parks, still a businesswoman of sorts. "All the State Board was men; the sheriff's office, they were men. I got the message all right: a woman alone shouldn't ought to be running a business."

"She was out here for awhile as a rotating ranger. Seemed nice to me," says Eva. "The park will still run."

I smile, but Eva's words carry the solid promise of twenty years of life here, and I take them home with me like the line of a song. It grows and changes in its meaning, moves from irony to consolation, mixing with very different thoughts. When we feel most desolate about the desert's future, Barbara reminds us both, in her own words, that the park will still run.

Somewhere, goes Eva's and Barbara's song, beneath our private fears and griefs at all the individual losses, flows the steady, pulsating energy of the earth, indestructible by men, original, creative.

Afterword

       When I gathered these journal entries together, Barbara and I had rented a little studio in San Diego, not much larger than our trailer. It brought us into city life for the longest time since we came to the desert five years ago. Those months in San Diego tell me how the desert has changed me.

       I see much more sharply now the obscenity of American life. On the desert, when we shop for food every ten days or two weeks, we use and re-use each of the few plastic or paper bags we collect. In the city we shop more often and, despite our efforts, we buy more. For the five-minute trip home from the market, maybe a dozen bags accumulate or get thrown away. In revolt, I bring them back to the stores to the lifted eyebrows of bag boys—another batty old dame into *saving* stuff.

Here in America's Finest City, children are watching their friends gunned down in gang crossfire, and the citizens vote to take down Martin Luther King's name and rename their main street "Market" Street, while the runoff from too many markets overflows in sewage spills and air that stings the lungs. In the parking lots of Safeway and Von's, I hand out literature from the farmworkers trying to end the massive use of pesticides that poison the grapes and the workers in the field. The response from the ordinary people like myself is: "Why grapes? Don't you know that all produce is loaded with pesticides? Don't you know the ocean out there is polluted?" It's as if I am mocking them with my tiny air of hope. My answer is some variation of: "Well, we have to start somewhere."

So we do. But we need a far wider view too, that the shoppers, in their way, are asking me for. A vision brave enough to shake us loose from centuries of the hype that swears technology has been and will be our salvation. A way of redreaming the American dream.

One of the persistent myths about "primitive" peoples is the terrible anxiety they endure from not comprehending the rules that explain the universe. Without the gifts of "civilized" science, the story goes, we would live in helpless fear of the unknown. Of course as word leaks out of the kingdoms of pre-colonial Africa or the complex astronomy of the Indians at Mesa Verde, we learn that the comprehension of native peoples has been conveniently underestimated. But sometimes I wonder how those supposed fears can possibly be vaster than the recent terrors we have yet to comprehend: nuclear winter, the green-house effect, death in the food we eat and the air we breathe.

Still, the instant we question progress, we meet rebuke for *romanticizing the primitive.* So reflex and stern is this warning that you might think that, through our folly, we were about to unleash forces that could subvert civilization and return us all to some vile, unworthy state. This while legions work through the night to romanticize washing machines, space shuttles, the miracles of modern medicine, floor pol-ish, sports cars, nuclear power plants. On the radio as I grew up, a sonorous, seductive male voice repeatedly promised me: "Better Things for Better Living—through Chemistry." Yesterday I turned on the car radio to hear a woman huskily insist that "nothing stirs the soul like the contours of a new automobile." In 1970, a physicist from Los Alamos told me with eyes aglow that, thanks to nuclear energy, in just twenty years everyone in the world would have time for the arts and culture. What agencies, what scientists are hired to romanticize a life of simplicity?

Lillian Smith spoke of women's "lack of *loyalty* to civilization," and our disloyalty gives us a power to ask questions larger than civilization. We may crowd to the malls, with our unnamed hunger and our bumper-stickers that say we were Born to Shop, but still our investment is marginal. Whatever the name on the charge card, we remain outsiders. Smokestacks, high-rises, rockets—these are not women's fantasies, and even as some of us learn the language of computers, we suspect that this latest social revolution will leave most women sitting at a small screen for low pay, our bathroom breaks monitored by microchip.

When I was a child, my father sometimes liked to concoct a gourmet meal, but when it was done my mother spent patient hours with pots crusted with hardened sauces, flour on the counters, grease on the floor. The space circling our planet is littered with floating junk. Most women know that nobody will clean our messes, that we'd best mop up as we go.

So it's women who can best search out ways to dismantle this monstrous technoculture. Native women, old women especially. They have been accused of resisting change, but what they resist is progress, for they know its price, have seen its by-products. Together we can dare a stern, hopeful vision—not of turning back the clock to a more naive time, but of moving it ahead to a time when we regain our senses.

Driving home after our summer in San Diego, I felt pulled as usual into the life of the desert, the reddish boulders and grey-green agave and tall grey stalks of ocotillo that no longer look austere to me even in our driest season. The air was sharp and bright, as it mostly is, though we've watched invasions of sludgey air thicken the mountains at times, especially after holiday weekends. But I noticed that the roads were newly widened, and here and there telephone trucks were parked in the sand along the way. New green telephone boxes blossomed every few miles by the roadside. I've seen too much in fifty-five years, and in the last five, and my heart chilled. A day or so later, going down to the mailbox, I saw a man in a telephone truck working on our phone. I stopped and called out, "What's going on? What are they doing between here and Shelter Valley?"

He came out of the booth and nodded to me.

"They're improving service. You're the end of the line here. Your phone service should be a lot better in a few weeks."

In the city, I would be delighted. Out here, it means nothing good.

"They're doing all this so our phone will take quarters?"

"Well, so you'll have better service. Somebody wants you to have it. They're adding thousands of lines all through here. Enough for two big cities."

So, after years of being no man's land, this desert will be "discovered," though not for what she is. More likely, like Palm Springs, as a new suburb for the rich, to be watered and planted with coastal flowers. It's the other part, I think, of being treated like a dyke. One minute the desert's despised. The next she's taken over like lesbians in pornography, prettied with makeup, a slicked-over version that has nothing to do with the passion and power of the original.

In these last two years, when the threatened changes felt unbearable, we've asked ourselves, "Should we leave?" But slowly we know: neither of us would leave the other because she was ailing with some environmental sickness, losing her color and her hair and her energies. So we won't leave this lover either, this desert, this planet.

But I make space to let the anger and the grieving sweep through me from time to time, as I would if one of us were dying. I'm teaching myself not to turn off that pain or label it *overreaction*. And maybe we will have to leave the desert to work to save her, but we won't abandon her.

For the first time in my life I feel my roots and they know their depth. They plunge deeper than family or 5000 years of culture. And I am comfortable with the contradiction that we put our roots down on temporary ground, with a house on wheels. Roots are not ownership, just as migrating people are not rootless. These years on the desert have taught me: all other roots, however cherished, are metaphors for this deepest connection, to the natural world, the nourishing ground of our being.

NOTES

. . . And Other Ways of Killing
Winona LaDuke writes of technoculture as a culture that supercedes national boundaries, capitalism or communism, and endangers native people and the planet in "They Always Come Back," *A Gathering of Spirit,* ed. Beth Brandt (*Sinister Wisdom 22/23,* 1983, reprint forthcoming from Firebrand Books, 141 The Commons, Ithaca, NY 14850), p. 53.

Afterword
Lillian Smith speaks of women's "lack of *loyalty* to civilization" in "Autobiography as a Dialogue between King and Corpse," reprinted in *The Winner Names the Age,* ed. Michelle Cliff (New York: W. W. Norton & Co., 1978), p. 191.

Cynthia Rich (b. 1933) has been living in a trailer on the Anza-Borrego Desert since 1983. She has published fiction, articles and reviews and co-authored, with her partner, Barbara Macdonald, *Look Me in the Eye: Old Women, Aging and Ageism* (Spinsters/Aunt Lute). She is a member of the Desert Waves affinity group for actions at the Nevada Test Site, and works to end the use of pesticides that are poisoning farmworkers and consumers.

▣spinsters | *aunt lute*▣

Spinsters/Aunt Lute Book Company was founded in 1986 through the merger of two successful feminist publishing businesses, Aunt Lute Book Company, formerly of Iowa City (founded 1982) and Spinsters Ink of San Francisco (founded 1978). This consolidation of skills and vision has strengthened our ability to produce vital books for diverse women's communities.

We are committed to publishing works outside the scope of mainstream commercial publishers: books that not only name crucial issues in women's lives, but more importantly encourage change and growth; books that help to make the best in our lives more possible.

Though Spinsters/Aunt Lute is a growing, energetic company, there is little margin in publishing to meet overhead and production expenses. We survive only through the generosity of our readers. So, we want to thank those of you who have further supported Spinsters/Aunt Lute—with donations, with subscriber monies, or low interest loans. It is that additional economic support that helps us bring out exciting new books.

Please write to us for information about our unique investment and contribution opportunities.

If you would like to know about other books we produce, write or phone for a free catalogue. You can buy books directly from us. Our efficient fulfillment department welcomes your order and will turn it around quickly. We can also supply you with the name of the bookstore closest to you that stocks our books.

We accept phone orders with Visa or Mastercard.

Spinsters/Aunt Lute
P.O. Box 410687
San Francisco, CA 94141
415-558-9655